What would you do if your country had fought a major war to defeat an enemy, and then 50 years later, most of your country believed most of what that enemy stood for?

Our Cliches Are Doing Our Thinking

A novel about 'young Germany's' ongoing 'war of ideas'
Marcus Sanford
Available at Amazon

"Environmentalism is the successor to failed socialism as justification for all-pervasive rule by a politburo of experts. Only now, it acts in the name of, not the proletariat, but the planet."
--Czech Republic President Vaclav Haval

And don't miss:

Nazi Oaks

The green sacrificial offering of the Judeo-Christian worldview
in the Holocaust
Mark Musser
Available at Christianbooks.com

"..an invaluable book for anyone who wants to understand how a rejection of the God of Christians and Jews led the Nazis to worship other, grimmer gods." --Bruce Walker, columnist

OUR CLICHES ARE DOING OUR THINKING

A novel

Marcus Sanford

Foreword
5

1: STRANGELY FAMILIAR
8

5 YEARS LATER:

2: THE MARRIAGE PUZZLE
15

3: THE SCOUTING TRIP
31

4: THE CAFÉ SESSIONS
67

5: JUST PERFECT FOR WRITING PHILOSOPHY
103

GERMAN GLOSSARY
113

"In Berlin in 1938, there were more rules about how you could interact with wild birds than with Jews."
--Pastor Niemoller
Died, 1942, Dachau

Foreword

If Hallon is the 'mind' and 'information' of this statement in novel form, Karin is the heart: *"What's to prevent these people from doing this all over again, and which people?"* That should be everyone's question.

Like Hallon, at a certain point in my research for KARMAGEDDON—'Young Germany's' Nature Movement, I realized that a few strange, occultic, psychic forays by some Nazi thinkers were peripheral to the matter at hand, and that the core was really the metaphysical unity of evolution and nature as understood by them.

The West seems to have been saved from dealing with all that (there are a few exceptions) because along came Heidegger who continued the 'total war' (war of ideas) in the sense of burning all bridges with rationality so that no one would ever guess what sources had been the driving the Nazi machine. To cap it all, he detested that they became a machine. But he never cut ties with the ideology. That, writes researcher Mark Musser, in the AMERICAN THINKER, should get everyone's attention.

As usual for fiction, several actual events generated the fictitious final story found here. As examples: there was a hijacking of an Air Canada 747 in the 1980s and the declaration by the terrorist. I called a Vancouver station about its tipline and my explanation of the hijacking was dismissed. Recently there was a group within the US military with a plan to disrupt the Washington state power grid and economy, in which the leader murdered a couple within it for speaking up. Heidegger was a regional university dean (ie, *fuhrer*) for a year, with further influence. Haeckl coined the term 'ecology.' There are books out by current environmentalists trying to create what distance they can between themselves and the science of the 'young Germans.' Nazi thinkers did fuse the two forces of Hinduism, saying 'destruction is construction.' British reporter Stanley High traveled extensively through Germany before the second Hohe Meissner rally to get a handle on the youth movement for his book titled YOUNG GERMANY. The Reich took over a state-of-the-art TV production facility called Terra Filmkunft, and there are parallels between director Harlan and Heidegger and their complicities. Heidegger had relations with some of his female students; among them, political historian Hannah Arendt.

All other similarities to other actual people or events are purely coincidental.

Our media and educational institutions tell us we are supposed to believe the myth that nature is nice and kindly since the Nazi episode is over; it is now 'safe' to base our culture and thinking on nature. Meanwhile, these same people have a fit about believing a miracle of Christ or His claims now that He is resurrected. More to the point: the Creator of Genesis and His delegation of stewardship is 'religulous,' while nature would never, ever, throw up another nature-dictatorship. And while we are on the subject, when the term 'stewardship' is used today, who did the delegating? The collective human conscious, or 'nature'? I seek the collapse of such a myth.

Many thanks to Zoedi Lepcik, Katie Jensen, Peter Wiant, Courtney Nelson, Stephie Hills, Rachel Campos, Mark Musser,

--*Marcus Sanford*
Near Seattle, WA, September 2012

1: STRANGELY FAMILIAR

During her college years in Portland, Karin Weisser worked the reception desk in the evening at the historic Cambria Hotel. She kept pushing toward something more managerial there, and she had the capacities. It had that international feel too it, which Karin enjoyed, because she had been taken to Germany by her parents once and it had opened up all kinds of pockets in her mind which had never been filled.

One was the black and white of grandparents near Freiborg out hiking and fishing. It was about the only thing she remembered about them, and she was really interested in finding out more about what they were like and what they did, but the details were really slow coming.

She thought about her work—or her consciousness about her work—as she checked in another customer from Brazil one day who was in the city for a meeting with Techtronix over in Beaverton. History, she thought. That's really what 'takes' me, and it is very important to know what captures you. Or detection, but not of a crime scene. That Brazilian man; that was just as interesting. How did he grow up? What opportunities did he have that led to him learning enough about oscilloscopes so that one day he was to be sent to Portland and attend a meeting? Was he a buyer, or a researcher? Had he come to complain that the Bx 1000 just didn't show a certain configuration like the RMS model, and why not, because it had all those other great medical data features?

Was she just interested in this for idle information or for the hotel? She wanted to find something that would benefit the hotel, and even thinking that way should impress her manager and lead to better opportunities.

But then one day, something happened that didn't completely change Karin's life, but it did change her program. Or it made up her mind about her program, and she decided she would get the certificate for teaching modern history at high schools rather than hospitality management.

A conference was being held at the Cambria, and it was some sort of planning committee for the state of Oregon having to do with a government mandate. She remembered the rolls of laughter coming out of the hall during one of the presentations, and when she checked the easel, the schedule said the session was about the legacy of Lynn White, Jr., of which she knew nothing. Just the word 'legacy' meant the person was from the previous generation and would be ancient history. It's just that a man had arrived with a friend just for that lecture, and he had Karin's last name, and a European accent.

The hotel policy had long since removed the last names of employees from their badges, so he would have no idea her family name was the same, like she did of his. She did wonder, like she would have about the Brazilian man, why a person would come through with the accent and want to attend that meeting especially.

But during the follow up of the meeting, with all of the some 40 people milling around, she noticed the man and his friend through the double door, all the way across the room, and facing her direction, while another man was talking to them. She didn't stare, but something reached clear across the room, some sort of bug or clue. She had an instinct about the temperament of the conversation, that something unusual was occurring—a serious debate, a disagreement.

It was the last session before dinner, and she completed the intake for another customer for the night. He looked into the conference room and said "Looks like a lively one there!" as he left.

The voices were a bit louder, but it was the type of voice that carried it, making people look and uncomfortable. Karin decided to step in closer so that the three knew she was observing them. She stood just inside the conference room but where she could plainly see the front desk, and met the eyes of Weisser, but briefly.

It turned out the volume was from Weisser and his friend, who didn't have the accent, but not from the man with his back to her. She had only scant notice of daytime attendees to the conference, but was pretty sure he was not staying at the Cambria.

Finally the exchange was over, and the one man left. She noticed his face, and knew she had not checked him in the night before, and he had already reached for the adhesive guest badge, to peel it off his suit coat. He looked clear faced, unalarmed or perturbed about what had happened, and was rolling the adhesive paper up in his right hand, while his left hand carried the folder from the conference at his side. Weisser and his friend were cooling off and one of them flopped down in a chair looking rather stumped.

Karin watched him leave and as he stepped through the front door, he deposited the label in the trash on the way out.

She approached the two men and asked them if everything was OK. They looked a little puzzled and said they were fine.

"Good," she replied, "There is ice water right there for our guests." They looked over and took note. "A Beck's for me, more like," sighed the accented one.

Karin then looked out into the parking lot for the other man, but he was nowhere to be seen. She peeked into the trash receptacle and could see the wadded label. One of her tasks late in the shift was to bag up the trash into a rolling bin at the back of the office, and she thought she'd have a look later on.

There was a Gordon Hallon who was a specialist on the Havasu Indians of California. But this was a Gorden. The searchbar message kept coming up:

DID YOU MEAN "GORDON HALLON"?

And then a whole slug of notices came along about locating people and friends and how to date people like Gordon Hallon.

She then tried Hallon and Lynn White, Jr., but this went nowhere.

It was about midnight, and she thought she'd try one other thing: Hallon and environmental planning, as the widest thing she could think of about the conference topic. But it didn't find anything about planning, just about Hallon and the natural environment, environmental movements, and nature movements. He was a philosopher of sorts, a writer. He was

12

located in Vancouver BC, and she found a list of presentations he had made at a seminar there, and in Denver on the 10th anniversary of the publishing of NATURE'S CHOICE, a sci-fi novel set in Denver, in which a government group knew how to survive an oxygen-consuming disaster and selected people to 'preserve' through it.

Nothing came up on Wiessen.

2: THE MARRIAGE PUZZLE

"Jordan, look. It's just something I have to figure out for myself."

"But, Karin, I thought getting married—I mean planning toward it--was all about open communication, or at least more open. You're closing this off from me."

"That's because I don't want to sound crazy."

Now Jordan was really stumped. "But, the way you're doing this…"

"I know, I know. You think I'm sounding crazy anyway. Let me put it this way. You're in your apartment, alright? Just pretend. I mean your house, but you're alone, is my point. Two rooms away you left a radio on or internet, and you finish doing something and you hear a voice. But you know you left the radio on. That's not the problem. The problem is it's a *voice* you know,

15

a friend, a person you know. You can't figure out, how did they get there or if they are on the radio, why they would be."

"And...?"

"Well, I'm right at the door, in my search, and it would be crazy to say they are *on the radio*, when they are not. I'm trying to figure out if it's the voice I think it is. In other words, I know there is the potential that something really substantial has happened that...affects all of us, my job, maybe your job, our whole culture. But it's just the potential for that, and its personal—I mean they *are* relatives—and I have to figure this out, what it means. And now, I've found out about a man—a research writer—up in Canada who has been working on this..."

"Uhhh, tell me about the man. Karin, what about our plans, I mean are you saying there is a 50/50 chance I'll be looking for someone else?"

"No, no. It's not a man like that. I mean he is a man, but anyway... I will marry you. I'm just saying it's too big of a question."

"What is too big, and for what?"

"The question... It's like being told all over, like my parents did, go to Europe, go visit those places we talk about, when you're just out of high school. Don't just go right in to college; and don't get married. Do single things while you're not attached, etc."

"But haven't you?"

"That's not the point, Jordan... This is...the next level of all that. It is a paradigmatic discovery—or it could be—and I have to find out if it *really* is and then when that's settled, I'm free to tie the knot, to make the home, to be totally devoted..."

Jordan was silent, looking out the window of the café.

"I'm doing you a favor."

"A favor?"

16

"If this is what I think, and we were married, I would be so gone." She reached for his hand, put hers on top. "You wouldn't want me this distracted and married at the same time, at least not for several years."

"Wow… You didn't tell me about the man in Canada."

"An author. Not a professor, although I'm not sure why not just yet. But if he's that close by car and this close to my topic—and he is—I can't ignore it."

"How long have you been in touch?"

"No, no, we're not on phone or chat. I mean when I *read* him, I know, I just know, I've got to go have this big talk. Not a big talk like you and me have. I'm sorry, it's…platonic. You know what I mean? It is a real intellectual pursuit and its personal, not because of any involvement with him, but his subject, and…"

"And what?"

"I don't want to say yet."

"I grant you that space."

She nodded. "It just has to be that way."

Gorden Hallon's stacks of books were becoming canyons. The phone rang. It was Sonia, the German translation assistant, and housekeeper. She lived nearby in a Vancouver BC suburb, and had worked with Hallon for nearly two years. Another piece to a puzzle was in place, maybe, she said.

Gorden thought that on a large scale that's what was going on. There was this huge puzzle, and like a translator on some rare document, he was gradually getting closer to a statement, a complete sentence.

He remembered when he first spoke to her, and her offer to be "on duty" for small tasks when it was such a staggering topic to open up.   Steady, systematic, unwilling to let the excitement of a discovery cloud her thinking.

"You see," he had explained, "in 1961 Mosse was repeating that a German historian was already lamenting that something was happening that was hiding the real sources from the public. *1961!* So when you take something this big and compress it all into convenient images in books and media, it's like the scattering of a puzzle. Maybe that's not the best picture. But it *is* like a scattered puzzle—the public can no longer tell what was there. No, no, it's like having all the edges of a puzzle, all the straight lines and thinking you know the image from that. Well, you do know the color palette, but you could be totally surprised when the image takes shape!"

He remembered when his children were young and one of the puzzles they worked on had many pieces that had been cut in the swirled shape of rounded swastikas. That was it, the picture he wanted his colleagues to see. Everyone knew about swastikas and that simple image of Nazi Germany. But when you put the puzzle together, you didn't see swastikas. You started seeing the formation of a very different image that no one talked about. So it *was* a good picture of what his work was about. The swastikas, the salutes, the marching troops—all very convenient and very disliked. But before all that...

Gorden was one of the very few people in the world researching 'young Germany.'

Jordan came by one Saturday. Karin made raspberry ice teas. "Jordan, here's something I can show you. See this poster? This is about the 'wild birds.'"

"The 'wild birds'?"

"After WW1, the youth of Germany were very scattered and disenchanted with their society. Many of them just left the big cities in the good weather and wandered all over. They hated manufacturing, loved nature, folk music, despised the older generation's failed war, etc. They became known as the '*Wandervogel*' or 'wild birds.' But see the poster?"

The longer-haired, naked German youth communing with nature and drawn to appear to be a growth of Germany's forests in the older poster were set beside a new age gathering invitation poster, and anyone could see the similarities.

"They all wandered rather sporadically, but then the word got around and a gathering formed at a place called Hohe Meissner in 1923. They called themselves the free youth, and they met for days and, well, 'figure out who they were.'"

"Well, Karin, there is a lot here. I mean that. It sounds really huge…and you've been looking into where it all goes?"

"Yes, I found Hallon's article and how he searched out a German historian who was saying it was all being lost. In 1961 he said it was already being misplaced, covered, hidden away."

"What was?"

"Well, usually when you hear about this, about the Third Reich, you are plastered with all the ugly and unlikeable images of what happened when it mechanized or institutionalized. So we see all the awful things they did, and we go, how did this happen? And so many of the answers just don't make it. It's like they just woke up one day and decided to take over the world, and to decimate the Jews. And so we've come to resist people that do that, that do those two things… But that's not what the German historian was pointing to. And that is what makes things so compelling. That and the relative…"

Jordan slid a little closer to say 'I'm starting to see what's captured you.' "So you've found something, an angle on all this, that's been covered up… And so what?"

"Well, a cover-up, you know. What else is there you need to know? But let me grab something for you." She left and returned with an article in a socialist newsletter for Oregon workers. "This guy is all upset about an author who takes issue with environmental regulations. The author was showing, plain enough, that many of these regulations—our regulations today—have their roots in German science at that time, that generation before the Third Reich. That doesn't sound like anything we hear today. Who would ever connect Nazism with environmentalism? Yet now there are books taking the question seriously—even if they end up defending the regulations."

Jordan perked up.

"Now, as this review goes on—the contributor to the newsletter--watch what happens: he starts insulting the author for forgetting all the usual images—swastikas, salutes, death camps—as though the author had forgotten them! And as though he had forgotten the article was all about the regulations. It is very strange, very reactionary. The newsletter *wants* the fractured, bit-piece, familiar-icon treatment, not the background. As though—poof!—nasty Nazis just suddenly appeared, hated Jews, shouted slogans in mass assemblies and had nothing to do with ecology!"

"So why, Karin, why has this all grabbed you?" He peered closely into her eyes for clues.

Karin tensed up as if she were being told he was unwilling to have children when they married. "Jordan, it was an awful thing, a horrible force at work, and those dominant images don't get to it."

"What is the 'it,' and what about your relative?"

"Hallon has a term for it. I don't want to sound crazy. Let's take a break, OK? Promise? No questions about it for a while."

Jordan was puzzled, because there seemed to be progress, but of course that meant a slightly different thing to him.

"Let's go up on Mt. Tabor Park. I could use a *dormant* volcano right now!" They laughed. "I'll put together some food. I have student papers to read. My head gets knotted up. Or goes wild. There's so much about this topic to think about, I can't concentrate on my student's papers."

Jordan thought he had it all sorted out. "Karin, you know what we need to do. We need to look up those other people who are a generation or two removed and found out they had relatives in the Reich, and, you know, see what they did to come to terms with it."

"I suppose."

"Well, there's got to be a way of going forward."

"But you see, Jordan, it's not exactly like that. So now I need to explain to you what I mean when I say 'I don't want to sound crazy.' Let's go sit in back." And they went out to the bench in the garden.

"There are two things. There might only have been one, except that one day, some of my students walked in abuzz about a street interview film they had seen one day. Over and over, the host asked people on the street what they knew about Adolf Hitler, and the younger they were, the less they knew.

"There was even one kid who thought Adolf Hitler was the name of a band who wrote background music for video games. He even said 'hitler' was German for a hit songwriter."

She snorted with laughter, but then realized how pathetic it was, and gasped, and went on.

"And then he went on to show the same thing about the 10 Commandments—in the Bible, you know, and generally showed that few people knew the significance of either and how those two things *together* could shape up for a bad situation. But you never got the sense that someone had *intentionally* told those interviewed people to think that way..."

She stared at the Portland skyline above her rose bushes, and then continued. "But this new topic—this is like the same thing all over again. This is the orchestrated, intended effort of all these brilliant scientists and artists to create a religion-sized movement out of science—but also pagan myth. I mean, it's science because the one who pushed evolution all over Germany was also the one who coined the term 'ecology.' But it's pagan legend because they believe they were created by the sun and are superior because of an extra-terrestrial electric spark, coming out of the sun... But why, why did they want all this? It's because they were unwilling to see themselves as a *converted* people, and they were desperate for an original myth in which there was an unbroken line from primal nature to today, and in Aryan cosmology they found it. It was all shaped to counter Judeo-Christianity."

"So? No one believes those things today. I mean no one believes the pagan side anymore, and all the extra-terrestrial people are, you know, staying up overnight to hear their guy on the radio."

"Or at least they don't do it in a way that sounds...*crazy*! It's all phrased now to sound so sophisticated and intelligent. And everyone believes the science side. All the terms, from ecology to sustainable technology to wildlife protection, come from those people. But even on origins, haven't we gone to the point where we believe 'nature' did all kinds of 'intelligent things' evolving mankind—anything but Judeo-Christian belief, don't you see?"

Jordan reached out to lift her chin, and observed the perfections of her face. "Karin, I have two things to say: you have a very graceful head, *and* there is a lot going on in there."

She blushed, and smiled. But she was staying on task, for now. "Really? What are you hearing? What do you think I'm saying?"

Jordan was surprised she wasn't coming up for air yet, and he just wanted to think about the fun of a wedding party and friends gathering. He forced himself back. "I think...I think you just said something that could get everyone's attention."

"What do you mean? Tell me what you're hearing."

Jordan tried to phrase it, and even though just a moment ago he was relaxed enough to go on praising Karin's beauty, he tensed up. It was not because he was not conversant. It was because he was realizing this really *was* big. "Everyone...our whole culture, our media, our professors, believes in nature the way *they* defined it."

"Yes. Yes! That's what I'm trying to say. The conceptions and vocabulary are all back there in 'young Germany.' Those kids (ahggg, I should know better) *students* walked all over Germany foraging berries and sleeping under the stars, and dreaming of a better day, and talking about the *Tao of this* and *Tao of that*. Don't you see...? All those images everyone has— except all those people in that student's film who didn't even know who Hitler was—all those images 'snow' us with...madmen, and warmongers, and even *Time* magazine throws in the word 'occultist.' But meanwhile look at how much of this we've adopted, as if..."

Jordan watched as Karin suddenly stood up. "'As if...'" he quoted her.

"Huh?" Karin tried to track. "As if it were 'safe' to delve back into it...so...they *won*...!"

23

Jordan was beginning to feel like the student who couldn't follow his professor down his trails. But then it settled in his mind. "Ahhh. They won culturally. This is not go--."

Karin shushed him, built a wall around herself, trying to grasp what had just come through so clearly.

"Jordan, I really have to go study under him, complete some tasks for him, whatever. This is what Heidegger meant about *total* war. He's got answers to these things. He knows what Heidegger was about. He knows where all this is going..."

"I don't know how you found out about Hallon. How did you come across him?"

"There was a PBS catalogue in the mail, and I'd been looking for THE DAY THE UNIVERSE CHANGED by the BBC's Burke on DVD. Sharp, witty material to use in class, and then I remembered there was this section that just barely skimmed this topic by speaking about evolution. The expected title was "Survival of the Fittest" but I remembered—these things keep escaping—that he was the first person I'd heard say anything like a direct link between evolution as believed in Germany and Nazism existed. Absolutely direct. But you see, the way he put it, most people would agree, but not realize..." A strange look came over her face, and there was fire in her eyes that spooked Jordan.

But she continued, "So I searched those terms together--evolution and Nazism--and up came a notice of presentation by Gorden Hallon in Vancouver BC on 'How Evolution 'Created' Nazism' followed by 'How Nazism 'Channeled' Ancient Paganism' and then 'How Nature Turned Yin' and then I thought this guy has put some critical thi--!"

She gasped.

"Karin!"

He no longer knew her, at least not intellectually. Like a midsummer sunset in the north changing the appearance of a familiar hill or grove of trees by lighting it from such an unusual direction, she now appeared to be so different from what he knew.

Her hand was still to her mouth in disbelief or shock at what she had envisioned. "Any day now, people could be praising the 'young Germans' for what they did!" She looked piercingly at him: *"We've been told so much about 'nature' doing this and doing that and keeping things the natural way, and a religion with a god is simply a joke, and if you do that long enough, and blast it out through every outlet, and arouse all the people with the wonders of nature long enough, and you don't even tell them about their own country's true history, and it's just 'nature' this and 'nature' that, and then you come along and tell them what the 'young Germans' stood for, and no one knows about Adolph Hitler, they are all going to join right along; can't you see?* It's perfectly thorough, in an evil way!"

"Karin, come on…I don't think…"

"Agggh! I can't think about it any more! Come on, let's get in the car, let's go find some music or something."

The band that was playing at the Palms was "Can't Take Anymore." Karin said "Perfect." Jazz and blues said the playbill. Karin had a Thai ginger beef. Jordan had pork ribs. Karin asked if his mom's therapy was still at the clinic or at home. It was at home. "She kind of misses the gang, though. She might go back as a volunteer."

"That's nice. I like your mom."

"The client from the call last month, the Everetts, didn't accept the houseplans after adjusting them for all the Natural Mandate codes. I'm not sure what will happen."

"They're playing something slow. Let's take this one."

25

Karin wanted it quiet and slow. Jordan was starting to grasp what she could be like. She was beside herself back at the house for a while, but she had made a good move and hadn't let it get out of hand. Slow-dancing was just the thing.

"And how do you feel about not knowing what will happen with the Everetts? Can you tell me how you feel? I'm sorry; I've just been so wrapped up in that, and it took me there, for a moment. You need to talk about your battles, too."

He didn't say anything about her moment. "You know, it's not losing *them* especially, it's the codes. It's a gray birch zone. Or that was one thing. They didn't want to plant them all around, and have people showing up in two or 5 or 10 years checking on them, telling them they could not do this or that…"

Karin had sipped just enough beer to miss that one. Or maybe it was the slow-dancing. Maybe, at this moment, it was just the thing for the both of them.

"Jordan, sit down with me." She pulled her chair up close back at their table. "You know—what happened this afternoon?"

"Well, you got seriously caught up in your topic!"

"But it was a sample."

"A sample of…"

She grabbed his hand and squeezed it hard to know she had his full attention. "I need the year or half-year that it's going to take to scrape down to the bottom of this, and what happened today was a sample of what it's like to be around me when I'm on it. There is no other way."

"Is there no other way?"

"I'm the granddaughter of one of Heidegger's TAs. I'm already half-way across this stream and I have to finish. How do you feel?"

Jordan could not say it right then.

26

When he dropped her off, she thanked him, "Just what I needed. Thanks for holding your questions. I'm sure you have a ton."

"We watched LIES AND WHISPERS, remember?" Jordan reasoned, when they met a few days later. "That was a lot more intense than this. Remember? *'My grandfather killed your sisters.'* And she wondered how he could forgive her. But he said, why must we be stuck in the past—or something to that effect?"

"More intense, yes. But maybe not happening currently. This stuff, this monism, this existentialism—this is how people think right now, by and large, and how they—I mean *what*--they try to eradicate Christianity   and other good things with. Jordan, do you see this clearly?   All this effort in 'young Germany' went into constructing an alternative to Judeo-Christianity as well as to *reason*, because they all believed those were 'outside of nature' and hostile to it, and for them, for 'young Germany,' that was god. And what happens when you do that? Well, now we know. And then comes the knock-out, as far as impacting culture: you tell people not to make connections, to disregard the history, you snow them with distracting images that don't really communicate, you engage in…oh, what was it? I just read it somewhere…something about 'intending to be forgetful'…now where was that?"

"So I'm not to be taking this as a personal rejection, like the woman in LIES AND WHISPERS?"

Karin left her stacks and moved to him and shook her head. "No, no, I *need* you on my side. We need to see what this is *together*… Now, if you can't see it, there's a difficulty. But I see it, and I think you will, and I don't know how you will get the background, given the demands of your work, but I'm saying, wait for me. I need to make this journey and when I'm back, or when I'm ready, you come and I'll set it all down for you… Do you see? I need you to support this trip, and maybe a move."

"What are you saying about us? About our marriage?"

"How about *my* work? Let's look at it that way. I'm saying I'm in the wrong work, and I don't want to teach high school students full-time for life. Besides, there's all the standardized interpretations. All politically-correct. I want to give my kids—our kids--more than half my attention, be home every day for them, because when my kids get home from school, *if* they go to school, they are going to have the best salad, or homemade soup, or whole grain cookies, when they get back. None of this hired-out stuff. But that's where this comes in. I need to go find out if and how I can make this the subject of my research and teaching. To see if there is a field to plow, and then what it would take to find a community college position in it part time—I mean less than half time. That's the practicality of all this. Beside all the wrenching 'ultimate issues' to chew over. I do know one thing. I don't see getting anywhere in this in the main academic circles, and that's where I need Hallon's advice as well. Anyway, small college teachers are better and have their small classes and close bonds; not all that mass-scale learning."

He kissed her hand. "I get it, thank you for saying that."

"Did I ever tell you about my friend Joelle, and the dog that arrived at her house?"

"What???" he fell back at such a huge subject change.

She read his signs. "No, not so much of a subject-change; you'll see. She was in the cabin on her way to Seaside. Not too many neighbors. One day in the winter, a dog is there on her front door mat, as if he had returned home, calm, attentive. A beautiful Australian red cattle dog. Joelle checked for any ID, took him to a vet for a chip scan, nothing. She put out notices, Craigslist, etc. Nothing. You know how she is about deer, and so the second day, the first group comes through, and Matty (she called him) starts off, and instinctively, paranormally, Matty knows she doesn't want him to chase the deer, and by sheer telepathy, he heels! It was such a perfect animal for her in her situation, that either a boyfriend brought him, all trained, or God did. And we know she still doesn't have the boyfriend! Well, she says 'I'd never have kept this dog, except what do you do when *it has picked you out*?' And so it is, with this topic.

"These things keep coming up, and there's an author to interview, and there is the relative to contact, and there's the vision of where it is all going—I mean culturally, socially. I'd be trying to find this field, no matter what. High school work is just a step to get there."

Heidegger had said that the movement would have succeeded if it hadn't become mechanized. Succeeded! What could that possibly entail, Karin wondered while reading something Hallon had mailed down to her. She grew ever suspicious of Heidegger's attack on clarity.

It was also perplexing that she was finding personal rejection from her peers at the high school because society's concensus was that Nazis were "right-wing, conservative nuts." She had now found very different material but there was no repair; the more she talked about it, the more she was marginalized. No one wanted to hear about how status-quo existentialism was actually the stream of thought of a person who never did break off from his National Socialist roots.

3: THE SCOUTING TRIP

"Professor Hallon?   I've just been hit from behind — not literally, don't worry. It's a training day at the school district, and I just don't remember notices about it, but I can't drive up today. They've made it mandatory. I'm going to have to…well, I'll just get a hotel and call you on Monday, and meet you and your wife then."

"Well," Hallon seemed to be speaking slow, perhaps disappointedly, "What's the training?"

"Actually, that's a good question. Someone in the state's department of education has come up with a carefully-constructed language system about offending people."

"Hmmm, well, it seems to me that we do a pretty good job of offending people without trying!"

"Sorry — *not* offending them."

"Oh, right. Who?"

"Well, that's exactly why half of me wants to go and find out what this is about. You know, I just don't get how they can throw in a seminar late like this and require it, and then it's on Saturday at a 'hub' school, and it's not paid. It's being billed as free Continuing Ed—so I guess they have a way of saying we're being paid--but there is also this…this sense of obligation or duty. Not patriotic, but…maybe for the 'good of the order' or something like that. I don't think I've run into this before. But I don't want to take up your time, and I'll see you Monday."

"Right. Well, keep me informed."

"Thank you all for coming" was the greeting from the instructor on offensive constructions of language. "You will see today that this is the kind of thing we must all address to work together as much as possible and hold our culture together. You are all aware of some of the historic decisions that are being made around the country, for example about same-sex marriage, and that there are traditions which are very different from that position, and so we have the necessity of addressing the problem of offensive constructions of language.

"I would like to remember to thank Dr. Conner for inviting me and for working on the administration of this seminar to give you free CE hours for coming. It seemed like the only solution, and I trust you will find that it is just what is needed. This kind of material will help us bond our communities together…"

Karin couldn't fault them for that. Obviously the word "retard" was to be covered. And the word "gay" when used by those who were not. One thing she did notice by the end of the morning was that two disparate groups were protected by this language along with what she expected to be covered. One was same-sex married couples, and the other was Muslims. The speaker was asked why same-sex married couples were to be protected from offense when so few people in the country approved, and he meandered.

"Well, then" said the questioner followed, "it's offensive to be called 'married,' isn't it? And then it's offensive to say *anything*."

The speaker glared back, and gave a short treatment on the waste of effort that goes into analytical thinking.

Another attendee asked about the tag "Nazi" which is occasionally attached to many different stems these days.

"Well, obviously we are not concerned about whether we offend a movement that is now 70 years in the past, and which no one in their right mind would join!" answered the speaker.

"So," asked another, "health-Nazis cannot say a person is 'fat,' when speaking of obesity?" The audience laughed.

The speaker said nothing about the hyphenated term, but thought the questioner was one-track-off with this syllogism: "Obesity is a disease, not a character issue, just as Islam is a race, not a religion." The audience found him to be brilliant when they heard that. "And I do mean 'tracks' of trains of thought when I say one-track-off. One train will derail, the other will progress."

Finally, a question came through, though the target moved: "Is being rich a religion, then? From what I gather here, there is nothing about offending the rich; there is no concern there; is that what you mean?"

The speaker looked around the silent group with a rehearsed expression on his face for a moment, a look of both being bothered that someone would analyze his remarks, and of 'how dare you?' "No, that's ridiculous; that's never been a problem."

And so, although they couldn't assimilate it rationally, this district of high school teachers was now clear on not offending people as they spoke to them.

Something she heard had arrested Karin's attention, and she was searching on her iphone, scanning web pages, miles away mentally. She couldn't drive her car in this frame of mind. It was so annoying. It had completely jerked her off-topic, and now, with the meeting over, she couldn't retrieve it. It was a demonic state to be in.

She went for a walk first, meandering through the dispersing crowd of teachers. The man who had asked about health-Nazis was talking with a friend and Karin heard him ask "So how can he say Islam is not a religion?" The question floated over Karin, and she stopped in the middle of all the movement. There was a moment of clarity, and she had to stop and capture it. *A fundamental category had been switched, and everyone had accepted it and she had this nagging feeling that that was what the whole meeting was about.*

Her Sunday drive north to Vancouver was over half-way completed. She stopped north of Seattle and looked over the acres of tulip farms from a convenience store. The view was great but the sound of the interstate slammed you no matter where you stood. She enjoyed a tea, and a bit of a walk, dormant tulip rows coming at you from all directions.

"No one in their right mind would join…" There it was again right out in plain view. Off topic, perhaps, but there was the cliché trap, or stronghold, or labyrinth, or whatever it was called, that had just sailed through the meeting about offending. The speaker had just made it absolutely clear, by going sideways from his intended topic, that anyone in Nazism was a nut-case.

As she returned to her car, a pile of trash in the corner of the lot caught her attention and faintly bothered her. Not because it was trash in general, and not as an eyesore so close to the beautiful radiant lines of the tulip fields. She looked a little closer and realized it was the residue of a meth addict's recent shopping. A pile of pill bottles left altogether suspiciously.

"No one in their right mind would leave such evidence..." she thought, and then the clarity burst on her from its unresolved status back at the meeting the day before. "*That's it*. We see them all as meth addicts out of control, out of their minds, dropping evidence right in front of everyone, and it's all due to those images—or the loss of much of the necessary knowledge. There was something really circuitous in that speaker's remarks. Why were those two groups the ones that were to be protected? Why was it OK and automatic to consider Nazism ridiculous? Why were the 'neos' that were around today stereotypically racist and heavily-tattooed? What if, in their day, the 'young Germans' were the polite, nice-looking mainstream who used the word 'solution' the way a UN spokesperson today might use it about hunger or water quality?

"Mr. Conley, the insulation content of the ceiling of this site is not *recovered* material. That is the simple fact of the case. It has to be recycled material from May 1, 2011 forward. It's an established part of the Natural Mandate, as you know."

"We haven't resolved the permit application date yet. Is it May 1 on the permit or on the installation?"

"It applies retroactively so that anything on that date is recovered material. There are several of these cases, these re-dos."

Jordan's voice raised with his disbelief. "Scissors-truss ceilings with mud drying? Did the inspector actually see the

35

conditions we are talking about? If there is damage to that, what is the recourse? Isn't this the first time this has been made a 'hard' order—applicable no matter what is the situation in the field? I just don't get it."

The scissors-truss ceiling was a wonderful piece of engineering that enlarged the interior space, but this was becoming a nightmare. Jordan was getting the feeling that they were deliberately finding such procedures to drag construction down to a halt, but he didn't go there.

The clerk had nothing else to say about it. "They are allowing 30 days for the correction, and then…"

"Yes…?"

"Well, then it's in violation, and you know the schedule of fees and so on, I'm sure." He pointed to the sheet under the counter glass.

"Now by correction, do you mean only replacement of the insulation or are you including any associated repair?"

"Replacement."

He didn't have the build of a scholar, as she expected when she first met him in the lobby of her hotel. He rather reminded her of Jordan. But she was a bit disappointed not to meet his wife, or that she hadn't made it. And uncomfortable.

"Pleased to meet you Dr. Hallon; I've been looking forward for quite a while."

"It's not Dr., though, but I appreciate the regard," he smiled.

"I was hoping your wife would have made it as well."

"We'll talk about that a little later… Are you thirsty?" And they sat down at one of the restaurant's lobby tables, looking up a street that gradually rose with the mound that shapes much of Vancouver's residential spread, then was horizoned by a mountain wall behind the towers downtown. Were the buildings out of place, or the mountains? The picture or the frame?

"Tea for me. I plan to keep as attentive as I can and chart out a plan of attack, I'd guess you'd say. I've taken a few days off from classes, and that seminar—oh, brother, not only was it horrible timing, but it pulled my mind so many directions, I didn't even want to get into a car and drive... But anyway, I made it. Why are you *here*, in Vancouver?"

"Oh, several reasons. My wife's roots are here, and its best for the boys."

"Uh, OK. I hope there hasn't been a misunderstanding—I mean about you meeting me here. I don't want a misunderstanding with your wife."

"No, no. I wouldn't want to be meeting there—at home. And this is where I usually meet publically. I have my case with me—" he pointed to his dark brown leather handbag. "There are times when we may need to be there, and it will be when Sonia is there, too. She helps with German and meals and with the boys, a great combination. There's also the monthly meeting."

"Your wife helps with the boys? What does that mean?"

"No, Sonia is not my wife. She's outside help. My wife-- she is, or was, an inspiration and a communication specialist. She succumbed to a strange blood illness a few years ago."

"Oh, I'm so sorry. That's a huge loss. Oh, my. I had no idea."

"No, of course not, and it has nothing to do with us convening here about your studies."

"Yes, I understand... Do you... Have you become stronger through it all?"

"Ahh, good question. This is where we have to have faith in something stronger than ourselves, and that God must be sovereign or else there is not a god worth having."

"Yes, I see why you say that."

"Well, it's sort of like Lucy's 'the more I grow, the bigger Aslan seems.'"

"Who's that now?"

"The youngest of the children in NARNIA — the Lewis fantasy?"

"Got it. OK."

"But there is another reason why I'm here, in Vancouver. In the late 80s, there was an incident on Air Canada in which a group that had the mission of 'militantly defending the planet' hijacked a jet across Canada so that they could make a declaration."

"The neo-Nazi's don't tend to do that kind of thing," Karin remarked, "maybe just hold small rallies, some small dinner-dances, I've heard. Or flip out and shoot a few dozen people!"

"True, but you see, the entire public impression of what happened was that it had nothing to do with Nazism, *neo or otherwise.*"

"What was the declaration?"

"*The planet cannot survive the human species; the species must be destroyed.*"

"Wow. I suppose they were just put away quietly and are still in jail. It reminds me of what Agent Smith in THE MATRIX would say."

"Yes. Some of their friends are out vandalizing equipment now and then, and camping half-way up state forest trees."

"Right, right. I heard about that. Out on an island, wasn't it?"

Gorden chuckled because the island was actually the provincial capital region, and came back to the subject of the hijacker. "Well, in a few days after the hijacking—no one was injured; it was just to get a national microphone—the RCMP had a notice on local broadcast TV seeking information. Or, at least anyone watching thought they did. I was already working on our topic, and called in on a tip from a friend to give them a summary of the background as I understood it. I could see why, then, there might be an edge on understanding if I was here, in Vancouver, where there were people actually in motion on these kinds of things. The hijacking was organized from here. And a slightly more European population as well. And then there is the problem of the American youth in their dismal educational system. These young people here are a few levels ahead at the same age. So that's more about why I'm here."

"And what did the RCMP say?"

"Someone at the station referring to himself as the liaison with the RCMP called back to say that I was clearly funded by the Lyndon LaRouche libertarians, and they couldn't really use me as a source!"

"Well," remarked Karin, pulling in a deep breath, "I'm not surprised. I've just been rather stumped at the write-offs from both directions that I find. Extremely powerful constructions of thought and language that control how much we are thinking."

"But it wasn't the RCMP."

"How do you mean?"

"The station, CVC, was acting as a clearinghouse for leads, but I think they were filtering them."

"That's sounding very suspicious."

39

"Look at it this way: if you were actually *assisting* the eco-terrorists, what would you do with all those leads?"

"Bury them!" blurted out Karin.

"Right. So it's quite a claim. I'm building the case slowly. Meanwhile, something else has come up in Washington state. Separate, but more ominous."

"How can you get more ominous than 'destroying the species'?"

"Well, nothing happened, remember. I mean, the claim is that the station 'captured' all these leads so that none of the helpful information would ever get to the RCMP, because it was lie that it would. But some details just came out about a murder in Nevada connected to a Washington state plot. The plot had two parts. One was the bombing of a 'major dam' to disrupt the economy, and the second was a poisoning of apples. These would lead to a few deaths, but it's hard to see them killing many people, just crippling the economy."

"And the murder?"

"The group, which was stationed in Nevada—I mean literally was in the Army and located there, but with plans and a stash of weapons in Washington—was going to execute these plans. A couple within the group was speaking up. The leader took them out."

"Yuck."

"But there is a bit more to it. Like I said, I can't say I get the effectiveness of apple poisoning, but the fellow was planning his own version of restoring the Columbia to the salmon, that is, 'restoring the earth.' He said he drew his inspiration from the removal of the Elwha Dam in mountains out west of Seattle, but didn't see why it had to be so expensive. And so there we have it—the violent restoration of the earth, which sounds somewhat like Wagner the anarchist, or like the 'machine-smashers' of the

40

late 1800s in Germany, many of whose children later became the *Wandervogel* youth. But it's also so irrational that it sounds like decisions that were made late in war, even lavish propaganda film productions when it was already a virtual loss.

"It is a rare gift you have Karin, because for most people the division between free-market and state-market is the most that they explore. This is quite different. This is the actual use of philosophy just when our educational and technological system has just about completely ended inquiry into philosophy. And besides, you have the relative you mentioned. A teaching assistant, wasn't he, for Martin Heidegger--at Freiberg, wasn't it?"

"Yes, Heidegger the unintelligible who never really left his National Socialist roots!" Karin blurted out.

"Well, you understand the point! It's too inflammatory to be that clear!"

"Yes, but I just don't know what they are doing with it, and don't know who 'they' are." Karin leaned back from the table.

"So what are we trying to accomplish here—I mean on your 'scouting' days here?"

Karin grinned. "Please don't be too surprised at my putting it this way...I'm here because my boyfriend wants to make wedding plans. I don't want to be a highschool instructor for life, and I want to find out if I can make this change now: to take this topic, get whatever degree I need to be an instructor in it, and work at a community college. When we have children, I want to be working less than 'half time' as they say."

"Wow...that's a very specific plan for you personally, and so we have to answer two questions. One, is there a topic worthy of mastering and presenting? Absolutely. Any college that has "Modern Germany" or "Modern Europe" could easily justify

"'Young Germany'." Two, will your Oregon system allow you the position you want if you have an MA in this? I cannot tell you that. You are in a metropolitan area, and you would offer — should we say 3 hours a week in it, meaning 10 hours of work. And in more than one site...I would think so..."

Gorden shifted and straightened up in his seat. "Now, tell me something about yourself: why would you decide to raise children that way if you could pursue a Ph.D. in this and go even further?"

"Well, call me what you like, but I happen to think women have a gift they are supposed to pass on to children. And I don't think this is going so well these days."

"Well, I wouldn't try to do a Ph.D. in this; there is so much opposition and unintelligibility. But we do need exposure, a presence. And then, if someone suggests it to you from the academic side, hey, go for it. But back to your point. How do you mean about children?"

Karin was at first surprised at the change of topic, but enjoyed his attention to the whole person. She searched around the views of the restaurant for something that would give her a clear image. "I saw a poster that made me really think about this once. Most of the workers were women; they were health care givers. It said *'People may not remember what you did for them; but they always remember how they felt.'* I mean something like that. We are raising so many kids who have no sensitivity for feeling, who don't express them, and what gifts women had for that are disappearing as they compete with men for work, like men. I only expect men to *try* to regard feelings, but women I expect to master them—all the ins and outs—including helping the men around them actually express it.

"I worry about our culture intellectually with all this philosophical ground we are covering, and about them emotionally with all the mothers gone from the scene, so that the most basic manners and treatment of each other is all 'caught up' in a freshman year class as 'human skills' or 'life skills'! As though we had no idea we needed to know it without a state-appointed teacher telling us! Look at any snapshots of life 20 or 30 years apart and all the conflicts these students have today were things most of them would have known how to solve back then, and mostly because mom took the time to teach politeness, consideration, honor."

"Very interesting. And it may not after all be too distant from this material."

"Really?" Karin asked with a restored excitement.

"Yes, families became passe' and were absorbed by the structure of the *bund* or *volk.*"

But Karin started about how she would feel if rejected for this material; whether she would just fight for it like a man, or would address a great shadow of unfeeling that it contained and that was moving all through the West in its great alienation from a father-figure god, as its depersonalized cosmic-energy-deity drifted all around. "And what if they cut me off?"

"Cut you off?"

"Mr. Hallon, people are doing all kinds of things to avoid or twist this topic into something else. You know, 'Lyndon Larouche funding' etc.? But still…it has to be tried…there must be a way. Maybe it is too specialized and needs to be at the state U. There are any number of edgy topics at Portland State, etc."

"And how about your Christian liberal arts colleges— aren't there a few of those in that area?"

"Yeah, yeah. I just need to think of a back-up plan, or a maybe a way to ease into it where I get up some momentum before hitting a rocky stretch of road…"

"Well, I have something here that can really help, even before you get to, or through, your MA."

"You have? You mean you have a project going that I can add to my resume?"

"I think so, and anyway, this topic needs it, to solidify it."

"This sounds good."

"I have my German assistant—and cook--Sonia. She has been doing a few things on it. Very level-headed. You could help move it along, and be a part of the team producing it."

Gorden stood up to stretch. He picked up the faint sound of a disturbance out front of the restaurant, and looked into it. There was a march or a gathering of sorts outside on the corner. "They're very vocal in Vancouver."

Karin smiled.

"I'll go have a look, and you could sit tight and sit this out."

When Hallon returned, his face was carrying an undeniable question mark. "It's an appeal for the release of the very eco-terrorist I just mentioned! Come listen."

They found a corner full of young people with posters and banners circulating. Gorden could think of no reason why they would select this particular corner, although many university students transferred buses here. As for the 'feel' of the group, Gorden found it to be as upbeat as sports fans. He didn't feel a threat just by being around them. Signage expressed their contentions:

NO HARM DONE!

And

HE MIGHT HAVE SAVED THE PLANET

As usual, there was always a niche of truth involved. But the irrationality of the second poster was double—the sort of messianism that cropped up in these things which, in other countries, elected presidents, and was so naïve about the workings of human governments and economies. Or naïve about destruction, in which they meant not the weakening of a local ecological system, but actually thought the destruction of the *entire* planet was at stake. *Principles without examples are platitudes,* Gorden recalled from a favorite professor.

"I think I see someone with leaflets, maybe books. Want to come or wait back in the lobby?"

"I'll think I'll wait in the lobby."

He went pro-actively toward the person with hand-outs. "So do you have a legal case or fund?"

The young woman with the stack of flyers shook her head. "No, we're not there yet. Looking for a case to represent?"

Gorden smiled. "No, I'm not able to do that. So you're thinking of it, though?"

Meanwhile a young man had approached Karin as she returned to the lobby. He gently touched her on the elbow to get her to turnabout. "How about dinner in a couple hours after the rally?"

Karin smiled politely but disinterestedly. She gave a safe explanation. "I don't think so...I'm from out of town, meeting my uncle."

"A guy gets tired of talking to strangers who are just going from A to B as quick as they can. I'll tell you our mission. Dinner's on me."

Karin was trying to hold onto this chance in a way that would put Gorden in contact with him if he wanted it in the future. "Well...within this group or organization, what's your position?"

"Creative consultant. Some on-the-street reporter scripts for CVC. There's the opportunity here to make a martyr out of Johanson and leverage that for The One. Are you with someone?"

Karin laughed nervously, but she had to sort out that acronym CVC. Where was that from? It sounded familiar. "Uhhh, am I with?--yeah, he's going to propose any day now. What do you mean by "The One" I didn't realize this was—you know—a cult 'with a mission.'"

"Oh, not in the old sense of Christian religion or even the Jesus-hippies and their 'rapture' trick. It's the *Tao* of nature, which Christianity never had any use for, since nature's just 'necessary evil property' to use and make more property. So what do you say? Dinner?"

"And so your answer—I mean this *Tao*'s answer—is to liquidate the human species?"

"You're quite an interesting, inquiring lady! What kind of work are you in?"

"I think I asked a question."

"Oh—the answer. Not exactly, but pretty close."

"Not exactly 'liquidate' or not exactly the 'species'? I work in specifics; there is a lot of misunderstanding out there in the form of images, and generalizations. So what does 'liquidate' mean?"

"I see." He now no longer knew if he was interested in this brain-chick. Her 'chick-bomb' had gone off inside his head and all the junk and mess in there now getting all straightened up, dusted off, sorted and put away, and now had the scent of lemon-lavender.

46

He was getting irritated beyond the resources of his romantic interests. There was probably a rule of thumb stated somewhere about mixing dating and politics, like there was about mixing politics and religion, although he was unaware that that mix is mostly what The One was about, provided you didn't think of it as religion or thought that religion was anti-natural.

Karin took the reins. "Hey, I don't detach my mind from my body, OK? You'll always get both. But if you want more of an audience, my uncle might be interested in hearing all this-- and I won't ask so many questions you don't like! Promise. We'll pay."

"OK. I'll get back to the masses. How about 5:30, here?"

"OK."

Gorden returned from collecting impressions from the rally. "I have this feeling that one day I'm going to be sitting down with the board of that TV station and we are going to have it out!"

"What...what station?"

"CVC, a local station."

"I was just asked out to dinner by someone from there, but I made a useful diversion."

"What? What do you mean?"

"A young guy from the rally who said he was a 'creative consultant' for them invited me to dinner. He said he was tired of catching the odd person who might listen for a moment on their way somewhere else. I told him I was meeting my uncle and that you might be interested. Yeah, 5:30 tonight, here."

"OK, good work."

"I just have to ask," interjected Karin. "How did you ever get started on this?"

"Ahh, yes. Well, I think I was just curious at first about the background of RAIDERS OF THE LOST ARK. Was there really a systematic effort to harness various kinds of spiritual or psychic power for the Reich? A friend said yes. It seemed goofy, and I think all I did was notice the break the movie made with the totally naturalistic explanations of things. Here was an explanation of something evil that went beyond the obvious repetition that it was simply a 'hate-group.'

"But it became more serious when a ROLLING STONE article on genocide mentioned some of these things. I think they even used the term *Wandervogel* about the German youth, but I eventually found that term in CO-EVOLUTION QUARTERLY which was trying to soften it. Then I noticed, as I recall, that even TIME/LIFE now had a book and video series on the Reich's leaders, with juicy little details on 4 leaders: a failed artist, a psychic, a vegetarian, and a poet. Maybe that doesn't mean much to you, but the odd thing was they were assigned jobs in which they had very little experience. It reminds me of Van Jones being made green jobs czar in the Obama administration.

"I came across Haeckl and Gasman's research on Haeckl, and realized how few discussions ever turned to the actual connection between evolution and Nazism. In fact, why hadn't CO-EVOLUTION QUARTERLY taken it up, since Nazism amounts to a *co-evolutionary* movement?

"That was really the most arresting thing. There was no problem showing that there were major 'mystical origins' as Mosse says, but I learned that many people were *not* discussing whether it was all based on connection to nature, and why, since then, had nature turned so kindly? And why was this 'kind' nature the new world-wide spirituality ever since? That's when my proposal to the American Association of Popular Culture was accepted, but I did not think I had a team of support, and I didn't have the resources to attend on my own. My title was: 'HOW NATURE TURNED YIN.'"

"Yes," responded Karin. "I still have a copy of the summary in my collection."

"But I do think that it planted a seed, and, as you know, these people are now scrambling to position themselves, writing books to qualify what 'young Germany' was about or what happened to Heidegger and so on."

"Now let me give you some details on the project that we can mutually leverage: here is my plan for this extended booklist," Gorden sat down and began to explain.

"We face a communication barrier, which is perhaps really an overload barrier. I'm sure you know what a link is on the internet. However, it is my observation that the internet 'link' has come to stand for something mentally--the loss of it. It is a little diversion or advertisement, if you will, of *another* topic that is just as important as the topic of the page, which at least gives the reader the sense that a summary of something he doesn't know would be worth a look. The simple sentence of the link leads to a page, and the page leads to reading."

"But so far, you aren't saying anything!"

"Well, I said it stands for something mentally, and I'm afraid this is where the battle is being lost. If an extended booklist was set up with the title and a juicy summary of that title, *but in a regular print collection,* not on the internet, the reader's minds reading the collection would begin to assimilate and prepare for this structure, this construct of knowledge to form *in their minds, not in digital collections on the internet or storage drives.* People's sense of the structure of our culture and world is being affected by the 'link,' because of those editors who insert them and *what they choose* to link to.

"I've come to think of it as our enemy, and I've devised something that works in reverse. We have to pick our fights.

You know by now how little sense people can make of the role of nature today, or anti-Christianity, and so they can't— intellectually—make the connection to its end-result. They can't see what we see because they are bombarded, not only by the opposite picture (Nazis are nut-cases) but also by un-coherence. Our minds are less coherent because, after all, there are links, and aren't links superior? Think about it: how many times out of 10 do you leave where you were reading, and follow the link?

"It won't do much good to put all the effort into getting *one* link up somewhere with a phrase or two that sounds absolutely backward by today's standards, chopped up by the fact that 30 other links want your attention. The answer therefore is the printed extended booklist with its one-liners to give the broadest possible *and undistracted* sense that there is an enormous body of material and concepts out there to be absorbed. But not too much of any one of them. And there is one other thing."

"OK. I see... This is good...and what is the other?"

"People need footnotes on cases like this, and when you think about what a footnote is, it provides the specific example of something said. With the extended booklist, we are one step ahead. We are providing a primary or secondary author's specific source, but then giving the widest statement as to what that book accomplishes in the whole picture. We are avoiding 'everything hanging on one quote.' The lines will be checked over by a screen-writer for enhancements—someone who really has the gift of the word."

"Yes, this is all well done, but," Karin thought, "everything is digital these days; I just don't know how this will flow out."

"Well, there does happen to be a way. I think it is called defaulted printing. Yes, send around the file electronically, but when it arrives it is designed to move directly to print form. The prompt shows up. When you're on Amazon or Ebooks you see those 'try a test drive' links and you get to see a few pages. Well, defaulted printing puts out 3 pages. At this stage, I'm for anything that makes this manifest—physically—rather than lost in the sea of digital information."

"And you want my help on it?"

"I want it to help *your* work move forward. Your name in the credits will be a great advantage that way."

"Why, because I'm a granddaughter of a teaching assistant of Heidegger's?"

"Well, that's our next corner to turn. What are we talking about? Let's see." He checked his watch. "I've got to be back for the boys, and arrange for Sonia for 5:30, for the dinner. So tomorrow, we'll meet here at 10 and dive into that."

"They have a huge smoked salmon Caesar salad here," Gorden proposed.

"Sounds great" responded Brett, the young man from the rally supporting the hijacker.

"Lovely" added Karin.

"So…was the rally successful?" asked Gorden.

"We made our point. John is a martyr, and we intend to expose the system for what it is doing. She said you were in some kind of research—what do you do?"

"Yes, I write on nature movements. Years ago, I proposed a topic to an American popular culture association— "How Nature Turned Yin"—as in *yin* and *yang*. It was a broad statement about how our perception of nature was once that it was fierce and full of struggle, but now—I proposed since World War II—it was gentle and kindly. Now, when you say system, would that be the legal system, or something bigger—the industrial economy?"

"Who says it's bigger? But we do mean to shake up the industrial economy, yes. You see, CVC gets it. The usual networks think they can invent a label like 'eco-terrorist' and that just by inventing that image or icon, discussion is over. CVC doesn't use it. They say 'environmental leader.'"

"But couldn't he have held a press conference as leader of a group and made his claims?"

"It's not the same. There's so much more attention now."

"I'm sorry," Gorden explained. "I'm just a bit confused. He really did hijack a 747 across Canada, right?"

"Yep, that's him. Gutsy, huh?"

"And the direct communication of that incident about the fragile planet is what?"

"Direct communication?"

"Well, if you had been at Cannery Row in the '30s and the herring runs were nearly gone, you could have held a press conference with the closed canneries in the background of your TV image, etc. Or the group that smashed the UW's greenhouses full of genetically-modified plants—your TV crew would have that in the background. But on this, I'm not seeing the direct proof or truth of your concern by commandeering a 747. Terrorizing thousands of people. Help me see it? If anything, burning tons of fuel in them is actually bad for the atmosphere, if I   understand   the   claims   correctly?"

Brett absorbed all this silently. "Now, what did you say back there about 'nature is now *yin* and used to be *yang*'?"

"There are groups down through history—the past century of scientific revolution mattering the most—that have said nature was a place of struggle and domination and survival of the strong."

52

"Go on."

"But now we have to 'protect' nature so extremely that a person has to commit a federal crime to make his point. Something's happened."

"Industry. We have to protect it from industrial systems. And if we don't, it is going to implode, but not literally. I mean eco-systems here and there are going to fail, all due to the Christian West's productivity and disconnection from nature."

"So Karin tells me you didn't get to explain that you seek, like John the hijacker, to liquidate the species; that is your proposed solution. I just want you to know that there have been groups in the past that proposed violent solutions, and it was pretty awful what happened."

"How do you mean?" asked Brett. "I understand violence being awful, but I mean the groups. Give me an example."

"Do you remember how you said you were upset with the other networks in the area 'canning' your guy as an 'eco-terrorist' dismissively, but you felt they had missed the point?"

"Right. Ticks me off."

"There are groups where the networks pound us with things—sorry--images, icons, sound-bytes, visuals--like 'hate-groups' or 'racism' and they are so effective, and repeated so many times, and they are so obsessed, that we see nothing else. It's like that comment about MSNBC's Chris Matthews—everything bad links to racism, no matter what he is looking at. He's incomprehensible after a while."

"So what are you saying?"

"I'm asking: what do you want your man to be known for, and is that coming across?"

"That he was daring, but harmless; that the planet is just that far away from suffocating; that the way to worship the planet is to buy less, use less, but I still don't think I've heard an example from you. And you, Karin, I haven't heard a peep. Do you see what I'm saying?"

Karin turned to Gorden. "Well?"

Gorden hated to be too deliberate because it was so easy to just slip into loud cross-denials. "But aren't you missing something—about 'destroying the species'? Do you actually have in mind a global national park with no visitors coming, because *there simply are no people here?*"

"No, no, there'd be people, just not these creeps that are 5% of the population using 50% of the sacred earth's resources so they can choose from 50 types of over-packaged junk cereals at the supermarket—anywhere in the country!"

"Now I find that very interesting, how you just said that, about the people worth keeping vs. not."

"Yeah, yeah. That's what it's all about, man. So maybe 'the species' is a bit much, an overstatement, a 'hijacking' of words but you get the point. That's what matters."

"A hijacking? The end justifies the means, you would say?"

"Yeah."

"Even in how we say things, let alone what we do in public?"

"Well, yeah. What is your point?"

"You know, Brett, isn't it kind of a 'crusade' to pursue some ideal no matter what happens along the way, what farms get burned down, what women and children are taken captive? Did you ever hear the saying 'Where they have burned books, they will burn people'?"

"And if we don't save the planet, then what?"

"OK, so you really believe yourselves to be worshipping the planet by saving it, yet your network should not refer to 'species-destroying' as eco-terrorism?"

"OK, so it's a couple of hard sells, but that's why I work for them. There's a way to get all this across. I'm starting to get the idea you have no feeling at all."

"Will you be able to get it across without dictating it?"

"Dictating? That would be *ideal*, and that's why I keep working—networking—with CVC, too. It's got to have a media outlet."

"So did you just say the ideal would be to dictate it? I supposed you would. Well, I'm not going to give away the examples of violence I hinted at. I just want you to know they *are* out there, if you know what to look for. And remember violence means you *violate* someone. People have attempted what you are doing and they turned dictatorial. Lots and lots of unintended results."

"Or intended!" Karin emphasized.

"You have to find them. You need to find them before you act any further" declared Gorden with some finality, as though he'd had his say.

It may have been merely the attractive female presence, but Brett found himself jerking back as soon as he heard her voice. He decided he'd heard enough, and he didn't want that chick-bomb going off again. "Thanks for the chat, and for the salad." He left a tip.

"I picked up some leaflets this afternoon and I might be in touch again. I know how to reach you."

When Brett had left, they sat silently for a while, and then Karin inquired. "So you brought him in so close to saying what had been tried in Germany, but never said so. What will people like that do?"

"Well, he doesn't need just one more person doing his thinking, does he? He's really got to go round out his knowledge and he has to know *whether* he has rounded it out. To be told this is what Germany or Heidegger did is just about an explosion; I've seen it a hundred times. All you get is denial. Well, I'll be off. Have a good rest. See you at 10 in the morning."

One of the first pages in her scrapbook on 'young Germany' was Hallon's topic proposal to the cultural association. Early one morning she went back to that, because she had seen so much clarity of thought in it and really, really wished she could have attended the lecture—which she now knew hadn't happened.

It was quiet at the hotel and the peaks called the Golden Ears northeast of her place were no longer dark silhouettes but showing shadows and edges and details to her in the window. She was impressed before she read it. She remembered hearing about a Golden Goal in soccer, a goal scored when extra time was allotted and there had to be a winning team to settle a competition. 'That's what I need—a golden goal to settle it all, or golden ears, to hear the decisive truth of it all…' It occurred to her that she was being prompted to pray. She prayed for such ears, and then some line she used to hear from a radio call-in counselor: 'now go do the right thing.' Then she read it again.

Abstract of
HOW NATURE TURNED YIN
Gordan Hallon, Vancouver, Canada
Submitted to the
American Association for Popular Culture

NATURE IS THE MODEL, or paradigm, of the New Age Movement. The most valuable way to assess the New Age movement, therefore, is to look at what previous nature movements have been like. Some earlier nature movements hoped to provide a model for a civilized, democratic society. But the very fact that nature was their paradigm was cause of one nature-infused elite to dominate all other people—and the countries. After that happened, nature movements defined nature quite arbitrarily.

Some minor figures, as well as the eldest Huxley, warned of the socially-destructive power of evolutionary theory as soon as it appeared. The social expression of evolution was itself double; it lent itself to both cooperative progress and to dog-eat-dog behaviors. But optimistic social thinkers in Europe and the US seem to have largely ignored the warnings. Evidence that Christianity and Judaism, both believing God to be separate from, those close at hand to this world, were impacting the market and the environment destructively are minimal. The practice of evolution, as E. Burke, shows, is the problem.

For the Germans, however, the inherent struggle in nature observed by evolutionary science was a basis for protecting the environment—if the right race was in the right position to do so. Proto-Nazi German monism was a struggle like nature itself for nature, albeit a romanticized German nature. In this view, a war could be a form of art. "The motorization of the Wehrmacht victory into France was a metaphysical act."—Heidegger.

Since there can be no criticism of the German bases for action in nature, nature movements since Nazism have had to redefine terms. Whether we look at today's environmentalism, witchcraft or feminism, all alike lack what we might call German philosophical thoroughness; they all deny that nature is both yin and yang. Nature is now fantasized about as though exclusively yin. For the moment this has some salient practical results. But there is indication that such a *conception is not arrived at rationally, and that fantasizing about nature may become a permanent practice, for example, a state religion.*

'This is a bit of a manifesto,' Karin reflected. 'If I turn my radio on, I wonder how long before I hear any one of these items contradicted by the standard writers of today's media, not as though they were on the prowl, but just as a matter of course?'

"Karin? Gorden Hallon here. I found out that Sonia is free at 10 to meet you and explain her role and also how the monthly gathering goes. And no, I wouldn't be inviting you over unless she was here. Then you'll know what it accomplishes even though you might miss the next one, you know, depending on when you move up. My place is not far from the hotel, a 10 minute walk. How about you drive the first time? Here's where to go..."

Hallon's office really was a busy worksite. She eventually found the desk. But that was after noticing a poster behind his chair on the wall from George Orwell:

WE MUST NOT LET
OUR CLICHES DO OUR THINKING FOR US

Hallon explained Nazi philosophy was anything but a simple set of cliches, and it was his mission to get that across. It was instead the attempt of the sharpest minds of that period to construct a fundamentally-new religion of nature paganism with the Aryan people as its purest expression. They were both its 'chosen people' (to supplant that part of Judaism) and the 'model people'--the end-game or objective of evolution was Aryans. This went on for decades prior. Decades.

"But" Karin complained, "I just heard an intelligent guest on a talk show about social evolution. He said it—democracy--would protect the little guy—that each of them would get strong and topple the powerful. He said there was no better example of where evolution was going than the US Democratic party."

"Now I wonder why he said *that*? The survival of the fittest would be the strong at the top pushing their will down on the rest. It sounds to me like someone was a little bit uncomfortable with the connection Haeckl made."

"Haeckl?"

"Well, that will be one of our sessions. Let's think about something practical..."

Gorden then explained things more personally: "My wife...was curious, intelligent, articulate. We had a wonderful relationship because we had no clichés. I called her the 'cliché detector,' because any time I used one about us, she would say, 'we need to talk.' We would sit down and realize that such things seeded trouble that needed to be nipped and avoided. Many years into my studies, I learned of that quote by George Orwell. They—cliches--really do need to be weeded out."

"That's very wise. Thank you, for telling me that."

Sonia was standing there, because so many books were on the chair. She was ready to explain the reference tool meetings and Gorden asked her to procede.

As Sonia explained what the monthly booklist meetings were like, he did rather want to talk further about what Karin was like. She didn't have much to say about the distant connection to her relative. It had all drifted away. But then he thought to himself, what was his mission in all this? It was to cultivate another solid student and spokesperson. It might be Karin, or it might not. What were the odds of finding someone this close to Heidegger ever again? But it was not to find a woman friend.

He had been lonely though, and it was a challenging topic, and finding a woman partner in his 50s was not like finding one in his 20s. He had wished sometimes he could find a Sonia or a Karin, with their deep interest in the topic, but he met ladies all the time who seemed to be repelled by it. Then he realized the chances of a "Karin" that was Sonia's age and uninvolved were even slimmer than either of them separately, and then he sort of forgot about it, as not worth thinking about. And not productive to the topic. He had worked with many people on the topic, many ages and backgrounds. And now a year was coming up with the beautiful and inquisitive and personally-related Karin several times a week. It was what it was. He laughed at the coincidences of life. He laughed outloud.

Sonia stopped. "Gorden? Did I say something wrong?"

"No, no, I'm sorry. I was thinking about something else. I'm very glad you're here to work on it, Karin. I think it will be a very mutually- improving situation."

Gorden added a few comments and was calling it a day. "You have a nice evening. I'll see you two to your cars."

Sonia joked with Karin about how a bomb had gone off in that office, and when she goes in there she puts on her miniaturization suit so she can get to the book or files she needs, unnoticed because he doesn't want anything to be moved. "We get along just fine. I actually know more about where things are than he does. One day he'll wish he was more organized, though!" added Sonia, asserting her role of being the woman in charge of the man of the house.

Karin left for her hotel. She walked around several blocks before turning in. This was getting really heavy. It was time to think about something tangible and delicious like croissants at a real bakery. And there was a real one, still open, its incandescent lighting whispering to her. She loved stepping in there, picking up on those deep scents lingering only in the air of an actual bakery.

With one croissant wrapped for Hallon for tomorrow, she held her shopping bag close to her like it was her best move of the day, and she walked on. At a corner near her hotel she noticed some commotion and had a curiosity but some sense of danger came to her as well. No, it wasn't that, either, exactly. It was a sense that she was walking into a situation, in which someone else's business was of utmost importance, and overshadowing her own, being forced on her. It was the tone of voice.

A young man was speaking to a small sympathetic group, and she noticed a few people would stop to catch a few lines. It was a scene like that park in Berkeley in the '60s during wide-spread student vocalization, or one in London she'd read about where unannounced spokespersons would address a burning issue, and the audience would either "aye" or throw messy sandwiches in his face. Then she thought it might be the same hijacker fans. She listened to a few lines:

You all remember, 'imagine no religion' from Lennon, but there's something Wagner had already started along this line, which was a new religion for the German people, based in the earth instead of heaven. We've forgotten Wagner was a rockstar in his time, and also an anarchist seeking the destruction of the world as we know it so the new world could appear. In a sense, he spread no religion, as we know it...

She turned away. She couldn't take in any more. She'd hoped it was going to be someone doing a live advertisement for a balloon festival next month. Rotten luck. But, no wonder Hallon lived here. She now felt like falling asleep watching the most useless television program she could find.

Finding people like that out on the street corner near her was making her feel like she was in language immersion. Gorden had said so—that this topic was like learning a language. From what she knew about that, she needed to do something for sheer escape.

After one further delicious croissant, she did just that. Some inane canned comedy was on local TV before the nightly 8:00 movie. She drifted off, but the TV was left on, and woke her after those first extremely valuable minutes of REM sleep. When she awoke, the story was a young, attractive, female professor lecturing in philosophy in an Ivy League setting. She was working on a line of connection between Kant, Heidegger and Wittgenstein. It was all in explanation of why we can't really know anything today in an absolute sense, since the method of knowing has collapsed around us. 'Propositional communication is practically void.'

Karin squealed and tensed and dug through her bed for the remote.

"His operating principle was that we should 'just be,' that we must forget the usual ways of knowing, and remain in the realm of being, of existence, of necessity..."

"Who? WHO? Dang!" Karin shouted at her TV, now angry that she had fallen asleep. The people next door thought she was a hockey fan gone wild, but there was no match on TV that night. Was she talking about Heidegger? Karin waited to see which of the three the professor meant and where she would go with it. Heidegger? In a *movie?*

"Intelligibility is suicide for philosophy," he said, and so there are no propositions to discuss, there is merely the relativity of language to discuss; so, in keeping with what he introduced, you are just to clear your mind of what you 'know' and just exist. Therefore this class is discontinued. You will all receive a B (and no one should try for anything higher anyway), but coursework is finished and there are no further meetings."

The professor looked around the room anticipating a reaction for a minute, but other than shrugging shoulders and sighing, no one said a thing. Then there were a few chuckles as people left the room.

"Well, she practices what she preaches!...Or what *he* preaches." Karin tried to 'store' what she'd just seen. The professor then pursued a young male student and talked him into coming to bed with her. Afterward, he explained he already had a girlfriend, and that he, as a starter for the basketball team, had been thinking of intentionally 'losing' games depending on how he'd set up betting on it from the inside. "I've got to raise money for my family" he explained.

"Brilliant" remarked the professor who dressed and left.

Karen was now ridiculously awake and annoyed at this confluence of events. She grabbed a sheet of paper and made some notes and called Gorden. There was only the voicemail recording. She groaned. "Dr. Hallon, or whatever you are, please call. I was just minding my own business walking home, and there was another, uhh, gathering, a street speaker about Wagner's religion, and then this movie, and a professor character was explaining Heidegger…"

"But it *was* about Heidegger...that's what I'm saying," Karin shouted into the phone to Gorden about 20 minutes later when he called back. Her neighbors were still confused about the rabid 'fan' next door. "The channel? Ummm, that's CVC, but I forget the tag name... Really? *That* station? Wow, so you're saying there is a chance that the station set up the RCMP line and 'filtered' response calls that were coming in, that it was someone at the station who dismissed you?... Uh-huh. I see. Yeah, that's smart, and that could be a great investigation... Oh, you did? You asked her if there was a legal fund and she said not yet? Meanwhile, they air the one movie that's out there that mentions anything about Heidegger and, no, there's no connection to him being a Nazi, and yes, everything decadent you can think of is validated by the professor of philosophy. And philosophy is now dead enough to be canceled for the term, because *'intelligibility is suicide for philosophy...'* Yes, I see. So, if one of the environmental protests is a news item, it's all rosy and venerated and upbeat... Gorden, it's all taking a familiar shape. Who was it who said 'God is dead; philosophy is dead; and I'm not feeling that well myself'?... 'It *wouldn't* be Heidegger?' What do you mean? Let me quote that back: (writing it down) *'Enjoy the war, because peace will be terrible.'* Oh, my God, there were German troops who actually said that, in the final months of the war?

"Gorden," Karin caught her breath. "I just have to ask: is this place like this all the time? The rallies? The gatherings? The movie?"

"It's very curious, isn't it, that all this happened just while you're here! I can't say about the movie, but as far as the other, that's why I'm here. So now I've got another reason to thoroughly check out that TV station. My mission, and my prayer, is to pass the torch on to others, and it looks like the

64

prayer was answered. I'm actually glad you're having all this happen... So what do you think? Are you going to move up?"

"What would you do if your country fought a major war to defeat an enemy, and then, 50 years later, most of your country accepts most of what that enemy stood for?"

"Right. That's it." Gorden smiled

"Here's some of the work that's been done on the extended booklist. You see, here's this feature I was explaining. You have the titles, and then a summary line like you would see for a storyline of a movie. Just read a few and you'll see how quickly this moves:

Sklar, D. GODS AND BEASTS: THE NAZIS AND THE OCCULT. Crowell, 1977. Sklar interviewed anyone from the British Golden Dawn (as in DAWN OF MAGIC) he could still find living.

Smith, B. HEINRICH HIMMLER; A NAZI IN THE MAKING, 1900-1926. Stanford, CA: Hoover Institution, 1971. A valuable subject by a reputable source. The value is in that Himmler is by other descriptions a veritable 'hippy,' and is also a researcher in agriculture, and the Reich makes him Chief of Secret Police! Discussion of Haeckl's impact on him about 'monistic religion.'

Stern, F. THE POLITICS OF CULTURAL DESPAIR. Doubleday, 1965. The despair that ultimately produced the belief expressed by Hitler that the war was serving the purpose of getting Germany back to natural conditions.

Karin thumbed through the current printout. 50 pages! Just of titles and single lines, and almost nothing she saw was ever discussed in her training in the US as a 20th century history instructor for publically-approved education.

She searched for an apartment nearby and began making plans to move up. This task had picked her out. Jordan would have to do his gazing at her on their weekends for a while. She had documents to gaze at, for as long as it took.

4: THE CAFÉ SESSIONS

"The subject of this session will be the images," began Gorden. "I think you've grasped something that is going on here, but I'm about to give you a tool that will—sorry to put it this way—make your head explode." He took a large drink of ice water with a slice of lemon floating in it. Karin was ready to take notes. She was drinking Green Chai tea these days.

"So let me put it to you the messiest way I can so that we can get right to the point of miscommunication today. Nazi Germany wasn't predominantly racist."

Karin stiffened. Until this she'd heard 13 bizarre things, but now her 'master' in this effort sounded like a wheel had come off. "OK...but you wouldn't walk around Vancouver saying that, would you?"

"Good point. There was something else. So let me tell you a story from when I went hiking as a child."

She liked how he would charge into the most serious thing, and then find some completely entertaining way to illustrate it.

"We had two car's worth of middle school hikers. We were returning from a spot 8 miles deep in the mountains, gravel road, low cloud ceiling, sometimes blocking out the view. And we were at 6000 feet, and the parent driving the first car out was the least experienced. The loss of view, the altitude, the dust, and spent energy all converged on him and through an opening in the clouds he saw the road ahead one ridge away and it actually looked like it was going straight up! This image triggered a panic attack, and he stopped. He got out and went back to the hiking party's leader in the second car and said 'I just can't do it! I just saw that road, and I've got to sit down' and he was breathing really hard. 'It's a panic attack, I think, from seeing that road. Like a person on a high wire who shouldn't look down.'

"Well, when I was an adult and up there driving, I could see his point. But one year I was up in that area and saw that same road from the side, from another ridge, that section appeared to be going straight up, and saw how really flat the slope was, and thought how incredibly different such a thing can appear when seen from another angle.

"My point is we have all these people reacting to images, because everything they are seeing is one angle. They have no idea that from the side angle, they would never react that way; they could then explain very simply why it need not lead to that reaction. But my goodness, we are only dealing with people's reactions to 'steep-road Nazism' and someone, somewhere wants it that way."

Karin was ready for the fasteners to be tightened.

"So, there was racism, yes, there was racism as we use the term today. But to use *racism* about 'young Germany' would seriously miss the mark. Let's say I'm your friend and we have lived on the same block for years. One day, you had no idea, you come around the corner and I'm in a huge moving van, all loaded and about to leave for another part of town. You ask me what I'm doing, and I say 'I'm driving.' *Driving?* That's what it's like to say this Germany was racist. If people find out Heidegger was at war about metaphysics (and that's what 'total war' meant), they'd realize you can only go so far from the Christian view before these things start happening."

Karin let out her breath, glad to realize the detour was short, if bumpy. Gorden waited. Karin looked hard. "Well, go on then, there must be all kinds of things going on that we need to talk about!" she said with some frustration. Where was the bottom and how deep was it?

"Oh, yes. Yes, indeed. I just wanted you to remember that story, when you're 'out there.'"

"Out there?"

"You're going to find that the image about Nazi Germany that is nestled so firmly among people who have at least 'read the introduction' is that it was a racist state, rather like South Africa. But remember when you said the swastikas, the salutes, the marching troops--all that was its iconography, but there was so much more leading up to them? Well, now I'm asking you to see *racism as the decoy icon which they want you to see.* While you're busy detesting racism, all kinds of things have got through. Even in Faye, with all his digging up details on Heidegger, the ugly sludge at the bottom of this has not been stirred."

69

"And so seeing that decoy means missing *what*? What would I be missing?"

"Viewing Germany as nature itself. Monism, which means the one reality. That's the *Weltanschaung,* the view of the world of 'young Germany.' Not just saying certain races had to go, or putting your race above. Quite a bit deeper—a view of nature as an ultimate authority, a god. But a pantheistic god. That means there is no god other than nature, of which man is one part. And believing that the Aryan's primal connection to that god was intact, unbroken, uncompromised. I'm assuming you know what metaphysics means, in philosophy. I don't mean a practitioner of some sort of mind-science or astral-calculation. I mean an explanation of ultimate reality—an answer to why anything is here at all, instead of nothing. It's cosmology, really. The Aryan *Weltanschaung* was that Germanness was intrinsically *nature*. That was the goal or purpose of it.

"As you may have found, this leaked out a couple times. One of them was that when the occupation of France was complete, which succeeded mechanically because of the speed of the *Wehrmacht,* Heidegger said it was a *metaphysical* act. This sounds ridiculous by today's polite and abstract standards, if they are discussing such things at all, but here is the thing. If these people, the movers and shakers, were just farm-raised country *dumkopfs,* what is the elegant philosophical language for? No, they really meant it. And they meant it violently enough for Hitler to say 'I cannot see why man should not be just as cruel as nature.'

Karin gasped. "See! There it is!"

"What? What's there?"

"Not only that he said that he was following nature as the model, but that it's snarling with brutality. No one knows today. No one knows nature was his model, and no one knows it's an awful model to follow! We just think we know because we can tell him off for being 'racist.'"

"Very good, Karin! It really that very fundamental. Go on."

"Go on? No, you go on. No sense in me..." she didn't finish.

"Sure there is. I want you to have fire. When you've got fire, you've got to express it. When you've got fire, you'll be pro-active, not reactive."

"Yep. Well, I'm at the right place. You go on. Please. More fuel for the fire."

"Right. Well, there are only a few positions about metaphysics, when all the dust settles. God is either there or not. He is personal, meaning he can communicate, or not, and so forth. They really believed they had an alternative, and they believed that because they refused to be seen as a *converted* people, with some other metaphysical position imposed on them.

"This is heavy, so let's look at an example with a reaction."

"Heavy?" Karin questioned sarcastically. "It's like, who were these people and why did they bother?"

"Oh, but they did. Let me back up. They didn't want to be seen as 'converted.' Now we know Germany had its Reformation in Christianity, and these thinkers, urged on by discoveries in natural sciences, decided to take it one step further. The Reformation hadn't wanted an Italian church, and 'young Germany' didn't want a Christian cosmology. They were probing back into the starting points and removing them and replacing them with the new *Weltanschaung.*

"Do you remember how the second wandering youth gathering occurred in 1933? Hohe Meissner, the *volkisch* gathering, the wandering youth, were now a decade older and ripe for organizing. Well, Heidegger, the same who gained world-popularity as a nature existentialist into the '60s, was 'on it' in 1933, providing structure. He went around to major German universities in key provinces with the authority to appoint a university *fuhrer*, so that the university had no further independence from the state. One of the rectors or deans who was dismissed for not being 100% Aryan declared 'This is the end of the universities!' Meaning, the end of free thought, besides many other precious things. So you might say, OK, so much for a few provinces in Germany. But that's not what he meant by ending un-German-ness."

"Now *that's* quite a term!" She wrote it out.

"But do you see? This was where the global 'purge' began. Not all the noise in the streets and in photographs preserved down to today—*Kristalnacht*, and painting *"Juden"* all over homes and businesses and so forth. It started in the intellectual circles. He said it was metaphysically necessary; that's how shifted the categories were. The planet needed to be swept clean. All because nature was now 'correctly' defined, they said. He was already at work on national standards for education in which what they said was 'science' would be mastered by elites for the creation of one identical inhabitant of planet earth, the Aryan. Why sweep the planet? Because they— the others—were *not* nature; that is what the *science* would say. The Aryan, however, was.

"So tell me, when you see signage against racism at, let's say the World Cup, on global TV, you feel good about the organization; and you should. But if you saw signage about 'following nature's mandate' you'd never, *ever* guess that you might be into something *worse*, would you?"

Karin responded. "No...everyone today thinks of nature in the kindest of terms—lavender and rain forests, etc. And

72

meanwhile we have Obama saying that 'the US was just like Nazi Germany!'"

"Which is rather selective of us, isn't it? And we have people saying 'my basic theological problem is "why does Bush allow so much evil?"' and all the category-chaos that involves. They actually think *that* is theology. But to stay on point: why have we *now* decided that nature is kindly?"

"Well, in the West we have charters for legal systems, and people have rights based in a Creator, which is a completely different answer than Aryanism would give to such questions."

"Yes," agreed Gorden, "But what happened to the danger and fierceness of nature—the survival of the strong, etc.?"

"Is...it Heidegger's confusion, his aggressive unclarity?"

"I believe so. This made the classic questions unintelligible, which is how he wanted it. Intentional unclarity. He *won*. He won the 'war of ideas.' He even said at one point that the loss of the actual European conflict meant nothing! But even the question of metaphysics, which, by the way, every person ponders, has been turned into a specialists' labyrinth beyond any use. Go get a 'course on disk' about it at the local library, and you can go two hours without hearing anything in ordinary language."

Karin sighed, speechless. "You know, it's really strange..."

"How's that? How do you mean?"

"No, no, you're perfectly clear. I mean...my parents had an old friend from Germany over for a birthday a year ago, and I was telling her about my next area of interest, my new interest, you know, what I'm studying her. And I didn't have anywhere near the grip I now have, but as soon as I mentioned a few things, she winced, and looked really dark and distressed, and

73

said 'Oh! It was so much worse.' And now I think I'm understanding why they..." And she stopped and reflected.

"Yeah, what?" asked Gorden softly, sensing this was a turning point for Karin.

"Oh...why they didn't talk about it."

They were quiet for a while. Gorden let it sink in, and waited for her to indicate what pace to procede.

Finally, Karin asked, "Can we, you know, sort of wrap up for a while? What were you saying?"

Gorden regrouped. "Let's think about our current setting, about what we can speak into it. I can't say our universities are really alive—free--as universities in the pre-Heidegger sense. Have you read any of the figures about who is hired and given tenure? It's pretty much identical. And anti-Christian. And global. The racist accusation is such a distraction, such a waste. I don't mean there should be any, but as far as what *Weltanschaung* prevails today. Welcome to the great un-discussion.

"So I gave you the example about the universities and Heidegger. Because way before the icons we know today as 'racism' was the intellectual position of Aryan cosmology and 'Ario-sophy,' a sort of Aryan New Age movement. *The universities, Karin!* Whatever the wandering, nature-loving youth had found was now the official theology where the latest in surgery was performed, where BMWs were being designed, where diesel was perfected, where the gates of Nebuchadnezzar were being reconstructed and preserved! You can't tell people like that to go out and be nasty racists! That's *not* how this happened. They were 'one with nature' as they knew it; they were romanticists; they had a belief system that said they *were* *nature* as Germans, their blood and their land, for years and years, and why they would actually recharge their souls by

74

hiking for a week, or protecting wild birds, or eating only local vegetarian diets—I mean recharge in the same metaphysical sense that philosophy used to have. And as Faye still hopes it has. He hopes that humanism will be enough, but I doubt it. The 'young Germans' knew you really had to attack the core components of Christianity."

"I can imagine" remarked Karin. "Actually, I can't. My head exploded a few minutes ago."

"Sorry. I warned you. I'm just going to make a summary statement. It will be on the exam."

"Exam?"

"The exam 'out there.' You've got to be conversant in this, or they will eat you alive. *'Young Germany' is not identified by race superiority or by its list of inferiors. It is marked by its unique and exclusive identity as* nature. *That's German monism; 'everyone else is outside of nature, un-German'.*"

Now she really needed air. Or water. Karin left without a further word, except to ask where find an aquatic center. Every cell in her wanted to ask, 'what's to prevent people from acting upon—or rather *with*--fierce, dominating nature again, and which people?' but her heart told her it was time for a break, for some DOC MARTIN, for the echo of children playing in the water, and water splashing, and sunlight and the delight of reduced gravity…

Gorden began to inquire about how CVC appeared to have posed as the RCMP. He found a commission which acted as an ombudsman about complaints about broadcasting. He explored what the authority of the ombudsman was, and tried to envision such a meeting. *"They both need to be there initially"* he said to himself.

Karin was completely rested when she lay down and decided to call Joelle in the hills west of Portland.

"What did Jordan think about you deciding to make the move up there?" Joelle was curious. "Yeah, we had a bit of a fight about it. I couldn't tell if it was jealousy, or career jealousy, or the distance, or maybe it's the anxiety of what his work is going through. I think he's settled down."

"I think you two go back far enough that you will get perspective and move on and be OK."

"Yeah? I want it to, but you have to understand how. You can't...live on clichés. If it was male jealousy, I've told him that Gorden is not interested. If it's career jealousy, he's just going to have to accept it, and I've told him I could wake up one day, years into teaching, and just ache to quit and cut boards into shapes and install them like him. If it's the distance, I can come down every other weekend or he can come up... If it's his work—you know maybe it really is just *that*. Maybe there's more going on with this 'mandate' than I thought. But there's that pain of pulling apart when all your thoughts are about the work and attention to joining. All of a sudden you're pulling back and separating. I'm confused. I don't like it. I was settled."

They were silent until Joelle realized minutes were going by and said "Should we just call each other back?"

"Yeah."

Karin dialed Jordan.

"I didn't want to fight because it adds one more thing that is hard to understand, and I'm sorry I did."

"I'm sorry I did, too. What *is* it? What do you think we are trying to sort out?" Jordan wasn't angry.

"Thank you for saying that and asking that. I don't know. I'm settled on you, Jordan. But maybe the 'mandate' is nagging you worse than either of us thought. Does that bother you more than the distance between us—even with our plan every other weekend?" She thought a little process-of-elimination would keep them talking.

"You know, I think it's this…" Jordan elaborated. Karin felt so relieved that so far no words were angry. "I had made a goal of capping a profession before marrying, and it's like the mandate regulations are specifically designed to take that plan apart. I just happened to have made that goal in relation to marriage, which I'm guessing not everyone does."

"So it's the 'mandate' in relation to the timing of our wedding?"

"Or is it the reality of your subject in relation to our wedding? I know I didn't sound like I accepted that the other day when we…, you know, …had words. But I do. I really do. Just like I believe you are mine."

"Yeah, I am, Jordan. I really am."

"Yes, I wish it was already done."

Karin recoiled inwardly, expecting a further complaint about why her studies had to move forward first. But she drew in as close as she could to support how he felt. "Yes, I understand that's how you must feel."

"Thanks…and…how about you? How do you feel?"

Karin really thought they were turning a corner here. "I… well, marriage is a decision that can have its own momentum and has to be handled with special energy…"

"Sorry, I don't follow."

"Children, Jordan. I mean, I could become pregnant right off, I could be sick, I could have complications, but I think you plan when you dive in. You have to have everything ready for that. The nest, you know? So I'm taking my risk with you, do you see, and it's scary, to think you might leave me, reject me. I love you, but this…I just happened to come across Dr. Hallon's work, at least I call him a doctor, but I see a mission for myself and I see a synthetic reality taking over our society and had no idea until I met him that I'm sort of related to it all. Not that I don't think that loving you is less of a mission—you will not be disappointed—nor our children--and I want many…but it's scary telling you all this again and realizing you might not…you know…you might decide not to love me…" She choked back tears.

"I'd be a fool."

"What? What was that?"

"You're smart, you're loving, you're beautiful, you're caring, you're going to be a great mother, you have so much potential. I'd be a fool to decide that. And I hope you won't see a reason to say no to me."

"Oh, Jordan. I'm so glad I called. I'm hugging you, you know… You know what else?"

"Hmm, what?"

"There's other work. Maybe you won't have to be dealing with that problem, that Natural Mandate guy. Maybe you'll have to be my assistant. Maybe you can let someone else deal with that bureaucracy and…just build custom windows or something?"

Gorden continued about clichés the next day at the cafe.

"Well," began Karin the next day, "I have to talk to you about a few things that came up yesterday."

"Things? Karin, we need to be clear about each other…"

"No, I mean people."

"Oh, *people*. Well, I'm aware I'm single but I just assumed that a woman who was intelligent and attractive like you had a boyfriend partner…"

"No, no. Not to worry about that. But Jordan is a bit jealous about this. I wish he was jealous about what I was learning. But really he's just upset about the timing right now. But anyway, back to people, meaning, Wagner and Heidegger and an organic German cosmology."

"Ahhh, *that*. OK…"

"Karin, check the list of confirmed attendance to this month's meeting on the reference tool. I just sent it by email. We've got a journalist who I hope will also help me on the CVC story and on that group inside the Army that was cracked open. Then there is the professor who is sort of in your same position. Wants to regroup, try to break this topic out. Then, I met another person one day just walking in the park at Swangard. I heard this German accent, but it wasn't really that. It was her demanding tone on people in the park about how they interacted with the wildlife there. If you'd heard her voice by itself, I mean, *really*. You know how there's those sound clips of German women commanding this and that in Holocaust films? Crikey! There was something there you could feel all around before you even saw her; and I'm not one to mention too much about that kind of thing! I'm surprised she decided to come but I told her I researched social movements, and in this case it was nature movements, and that some have even said their group and nature itself are inseparable, identical. She was interested. And Sonia of course, as a sort of secretary, and her husband."

"Wow, this is really something. But how does this help get the booklist done?"

"Well, I do want the in-person reactions and want to push the front edge of how we are talking about things, how we are saying things. We want to screen out clichés, and we don't want any baggage in the way of clarity, and we want to make it readable to that younger generation."

"OK, I see how you mean. Looking forward to it."

"See you here, then."

"I've decided how I want to approach this," Gorden explained to the telecommunications ombudsman, "And it's this: I want a public relations representative from the RCMP present at our first meeting." These people never look like what you are expecting them to look like, Gordon thought. And that was really true this time.

"The RCMP? But that's the party to whom the information was intended to arrive, wasn't it?"

"Yes, it's just that I want—from our first meeting—for the parties to know what I'm saying *with feedback* so that there is no mistaking things about what I believe happened. If what I think happened is true, the RCMP will have their own reason to take it up from that point on."

"Well, it is a bit unusual, but if you're just asking for it from the first meeting, we can manage that."

"Thank you."

"May I ask, 'Why are you engaging them outside provincial court?'"

"I just want to make sure there hasn't been a simple misunderstanding. That's all. I would think it was rather strange to have an ombudsman contact me about some party who had an issue with me without some contact with them first. So I'm meeting them this way because you oversee telecommunications and it affects them, and the federal police of course."

The meeting was set for the next week, and hosted by the ombudsman in a federal building meeting room downtown.

There was no air of tension about it, as the spokesperson from CVC had no idea what the issue was, nor did the officer from the RCMP.

The ombudsman opened the meeting by saying that Mr. Hallon had requested a private audience of his question with the parties involved to see if he had misunderstood the incident. He was introduced as a researcher on 'social movements, especially those embracing nature and the environment' and since the incident related to a hijacking by one of those willing to take serious risks, and wishing to gain national attention, the meeting was relevant to all parties invited.

"When the hijacking occurred," began Gorden, "I didn't think of any connection to any nature movement, peaceful or radical, as I'm sure none of you did. But then the details came through and John the spokesman was given the opportunity to explain himself with the declaration about 'ending the species' which I'm sure needs no repetition.

"I followed this up when a friend noticed a 'tip line' advertised on CVC where information regarding the incident could be called in. While it was not the RCMP itself, it had the appeal that the information would be useful to them. I believe you can check the records of other stations and find that no other Vancouver station had this ad running.

"Let's say it was legitimate--and that is not my place to decide--I just want to explain what happened when I called in. I gave very little introduction to my work, and simply said that I was researching the topic because of the vast amount of material that shows that Nazi philosophy was making such fundamental declarations as well.

"I was then dismissed as belonging to some libertarian party--and an American one that--and that my information would be of no use. I will repeat everything I've said here under oath if it comes to that. The problem is I don't have the name of the liaison, but I would think the problem for the three of you would be something like the chain-of-evidence, and/or the policies about how to handle such calls."

The CVC representative spoke immediately and nervously saying that he could not say anything on behalf of the station without his attorney present. The ombudsman said there definitely were policies that had to be checked about how tip-lines are approved, and the RCMP officer declared "I think there is at least an investigation here. Maybe more. I can tell you that this kind of thing normally moves a case from the frig back to the stovetop."

"Now, on Faye, we really want to circulate the summary line all around and get the sharpest thing we can." The monthly face-time gathering to coordinate effort on the extended booklist had been going about an hour. Gorden was referring to the new study on Martin Heidegger by French scholar Immanuel Faye. Faye had gone through Heidegger's seminar papers and shown very clearly that terms like 'being' and 'necessity' and 'care' in Heidegger, were connected to existentialism by world-wide media. But while they were not connected to Nazi philosophy by shear silence and non-discussion, they were very clearly his way of carrying on Nazi philosophy. It was Nazi thought made 'soft' or 'lite.' Obviously it wouldn't be violent; it might even be anti-war. And on the Jewish question, well, Nazi philosophy would never get anywhere there. "But you can see how the intention is to have the entire society pick up this way of thinking. We just don't know who the victims would be.

"And can I just add what we don't know, which is the most perplexing about all this: what's to stop it from punishing and eliminating those who are deemed useless, inferior, 'un-real,' etc.? I still don't know."

"We have one item here from the national Canadian network CBC called 'Karmageddon?'" announced Sonia, believing the material had been covered enough for the time being. "A 'success' cult or church is interviewed. They seemed to be quite jealous of successful Jews, and had an admiration for Hitler's belief in what was *karma* for the Jews. That's a bit of a different angle, but useful... Wasn't there—didn't we already have an item like this called THE INDO-ARYAN RENAISSANCE by an obscure author in California? It's sounding like this needs to be grouped together or linked to each other."

"Now be careful with that word *link*," cut in Gorden, and the regulars laughed, knowing his mission about real reading.

Karin had the current draft of the booklist. A person could look a title and work back to the author, and find a summary or a remark under the author-based listing.

"Here's one we need to have summarized: MONISM AS THE GOAL OF CIVILIZATION, by W. Ostwald," Sonia continued. "This is a primary source, and it would be hard to get closer to a self-declaration than that! It was published by an international committee for monism, which of course was located in Hamburg, and of which Haeckl was founding chairman."

"Excellent," remarked Gordon. "And now I would like to see what our guest has to say tonight—Eva? Is this all new ground to you?"

"Yes, I'm quite a bit shocked at what I'm hearing, you know," replied Eva who had restrained her usual assertive trait, which she needed for dealing with the public in the park. Her German accent made clear how she was raised. "I believe I was raised only to react to the end-game or end-result of 'Holocaust,' which everyone disdains these days, unless you are a member of some strange cult or militia, and so on."

"I think that's quite true, Eva," Gorden concurred to increase her sense of comfort at speaking about it. "Thank you for saying that. Go on."

"But now I realize—I mean, look at your work, the size of this booklist, the title after title—there is or was so much going into this, and yes, who would want to talk about it. But you have to talk about it to know that there were steps on the way there, and why they made 'sense' to the people at the time."

"Do you think there are things that would have made sense to you if you had lived then?" inquired Gorden.

"Ooooh, now that's really hard!" Eva's face began to storm in some anger at being asked so directly. "What can I say? I only have my own frame of reference, you know, what I have grown up in, and I don't know what to do with what you're saying. I would say I have grown up serving nature and maybe to the point of being an enforcer for it, a policeman, to the point"—and her voice broke—"I've lost two boyfriends over it, I think. It's odd how attracted you can be to someone who eventually just hates what you think is your mission, and *not* attracted to those who are on your same mission. One of them even said I sound like a dictator." Her eyes watered and she wiped them.

"And now that you've heard of some of this material, what do you think you'll do?"

"Well, I will really have to do some thinking about that. I don't know what I will do. I'll be doing some reading. As for my parents, you know, there isn't very much about this that they talked about. I don't know what will happen."

Nothing could have prepared Gorden for what he found next. He had begun to look into how the media operated during the Reich, and how the whole controversy about the filmmaker Harlan was starting to look just like Heidegger's own progression through post-war life. They may have disagreed on the extent to which they were forced to function for the Reich (or on their recollection of it), but they were both deeply involved.

The main production center of the time was Berlin Film GMBH. However, that was the name of it during the Reich when acquired. It had been taken over from Terra Filmkunft which was an Austrian investment. *Earth Studios!* Gorden was astounded. He dug around in old documents for the name of the investing company and then it all fell into place. *The same investment firm had established CVC!* Well, of course, he thought. And now the sludge was starting to be stirred up. The station ran all the avant-garde programs, featured all the leaders of diverse social and sexual groups, warmly welcomed spokespersons for same-sex marriage, showed the one film out there that mentions anything about Heidegger, regularly mocked anything that came along about Christianity. It now appeared to have set-up and filtered a mock-RCMP attempt to collect information on an eco-terrorist group which believed the human species was to be liquidated.

He watched a newer German documentary on Harlan and the media 'culture' was all there. The kind of Hollywood superiority and arrogance was there in the production culture, the divorces, the splashy headlines, the connection to *chic* industry. They were all part of the machinery of the Reich. And it was all nearly the exact opposite of any sampling of Nazi culture a person would see in today's media and literature.

Gorden was profoundly baffled.

Gorden came back to the Orwellian saying. They decided to try Hibiscus Green Coffee, one of those newer energy drinks.

"Look," cried Karin, "a *green* energy drink!"

"Hmm," noticed Gorden, "I wonder how I'll sound drinking *that!*" They laughed.

"Once you see that we have let our clichés do our thinking, in history, in philosophy, in church, and you really look past Heidegger's gasping attacks on 'knowledge' in Nazi philosophy, you see both why he was so aggressively cloudy, and why there is such a huge cost for our academia and media if people know that Nazi philosophy is more than a few clichés acted upon by mindless, tattoo-plastered 'goons.' Anti-Christianity is by necessity anti-Judeo-Christianity and so there you have the Jewish 'problem.' But so much more of the world-view has come through. Nazism took a different tack when it came to Christianity. They attempted to evolve it or supercede what we know with an Aryan Gospel, which means they only attempted to destroy it on paper, not an actual holocaust."

"OK, now," Karin stood up for a moment. "The part I get the least here is about Christianity. I've...lost my grip there. I notice a movie every couple years... But what I need is a handle for it that matters here."

"But we do need to come back to 'holocaust,' because once again, maybe because of the movie, we 'see' or 'think' in terms of the end product, which was awful. You know, gassing and burning people. But the cause was offering."

"Offering? You're not being clear," Karin complained.

"Holocaust is not a term that originates with the Jews describing what happened. It was the intended offering by Aryanism."

"An offering?"

"An act of worship."

"Dr. Hallon!" Karin was upset at what was unfolding.

"What?"

"So--who is the 'god' they were offering to?" Karin was breathing hard and squirming.

"We're getting there, Karin. I...have to provide some background about Christianity because without that you can't understand the *total* war."

"Now that expression I did hear about—oh, where was that?"

"Not to worry," assured Gorden. "Just let it build slowly. It will come together. So as a world view—a *Weltanschaung*—I can make those points about Christianity. A really good treatment of Judeo-Christianity came out after Lewis, which was Dr. Schaeffer writing on 'He is there and he is not silent.' That simply asserts (that is, to reflect his account in a fresh way) He—God—is a person like us, but infinite, and communicates with us, though not everything He could. I insert the term Judeo- so that you will make the necessary connection to the friction with the Jews. It was a *world view* conflict first. And, by the way, Dr. Schaeffer went to Frieborg to speak in 1967."

"Oh, wow!" exclaimed Karin, and wondering how all that went.

"Now, I have mentioned that the opposition to Christianity is what explains anti-semitism, because it is really anti-Judeo-Christianity. But there is another piece to the machinery to notice right here. There is opposition to reason. Unlike today, these thinkers realized that Christianity was highly reasonable. They knew this from various statements by Paul in *Romans* and *Acts*. In their reactive mentality, then, they had to explode both. That's why, as you can see from the booklist, the mystical, the superstitious, the irrational, the occult comes flooding in to replace all that. Today people just assume any talk of Christianity is a non-sensical discussion. Not so at that time; reason *itself* had to be destroyed and replaced by instincts and intuitions."

"Gorden," Karin interrupted. "I've never asked: what was Heidegger trained in?"

"Good question. He was a theologian, and so you can imagine two things: one, that he would know what Judeo-Christianity was really saying, and two, that he would be in a position to write material opposed to it in such fundamental categories so as to make room for a completely new and German system."

"They really brought in all types, didn't they—agriculture research, painters, mystics…?"

"Yes, it's quite a range. You'll find the problem with a rational Christianity addressed right in the romantic life of Goethe. And maybe it was a bit too academic. But now back to the fundamental categories. Most people hear the word 'infinite' and go immediately to their objections: 'what about God and evil? Or can He make a mountain He can't lift, etc.?'—which we won't take up now, except one thing. The Judeo-Christian account says there was an invasion of evil, that mankind joined it, and that is separate from God, so that God can be angry at evil *without being angry at Himself,* which is the dilemma so many philosophers have tried to exploit to undercut Christianity.

"Then there is law, which Christianity's teachers have said is essentially known by all people. 'Love your neighbor as yourself' implies that.

"Then there is its Gospel, which is how it addresses the human shortcoming as a debt to be reconciled.

"But our question would now be: what is it that Aryanism wished to say about all this? There are a few peripheral things like the meek Jesus they reject in their '5th

Gospel' as not being warrior enough. But essentially they reject a personal and distinct God because they believed themselves *to be nature*, which was an impersonal and indistinct god. They were pantheist, pulling in pagan concepts from all over.

"You asked 'to whom was the holocaust offered?' Well, it was a pantheistic god—nature itself. Hitler said once that 'in National Socialism, mankind is becoming god.' They were what Christian theologians would call pre-lapsarian about nature— they believed there was nothing evil about it; it was just 'there'— Heidegger would say it was 'Being,' but with another twist: As though we now live before (pre) the evil change (lapse). You'll hear this in Heidegger. Actually, he'll say the lapse was rationality, and that's why an alliance between reason *and* Judeo-Christianity was the enemy, and why in part he is an existentialist theologian. He dates this to Aristotle, but that sort of falls apart.

"But when Dr. Schaeffer talks about the existentialist person living in an apparently meaningless world, let's put on Heidegger's glasses. Translation: 'the un-natural peoples of the world, the ones who are not in essence nature themselves, have us doing all kinds of things we don't want and don't value. Total war on them! Ideas and bodies must burn!'"

Karin was writing another one of Gorden's big invented words (or so she thought) and burst in: "P-R-E-L-A-P-S-A-R-I-A-N. And '–arian' got in there too!"

"Good try, but just a coincidence! I suppose people will debate forever whether their superiority-complex came first or not, but it was clearly much easier to turn nature into a supportive framework for Aryanism than Judeo-Christianity. Do you see that? So you will hear about Ayro-sophy, more than Aryan Christianity. Because Judeo-Christianity's opening chapters make it clear that God, man, and nature are all quite distinct. That's what Heidegger meant about rejecting any 'revealed truth' or human reason, and just 'existing.'"

Gorden looked at her as if to measure her alertness: "You do understand about the term 'holocaust' right?"

"How do you mean?"

"It's their offering to the sun, who created primal Aryans—so they say--with electro-shock impulses... Not that we are to think of the literal sun, but the god they imagined. But my concern is simply the anti-Christianity dimension. They were burning all those people...to honor their belief." His fluid voice took a serious turn. "*We must realize that departure from Christianity is to go into a dark irrationality whose credit rating is bankrupt.* It was Rosenberg, as I recall, who oversaw the annual summer solstice high-noon hour of silence, with all the youth marshaled in formation in honor of their 'creator.'"

Karin calculated. "So that departure, that anti-Christianity, would include all the forces today that marginalize Judeo-Christianity—that would mean..."

"And marginalize rationality..."

"But why does Nazism look so mechanized, organized, regimented—and why do we have this strong reaction to it as 'conservative'?"

"Well, as they got older and formed a political party they realized one thing: being a-political would never get anything accomplished. Hitler was too politically shrewd to miss that. So organization came back with a vengeance. To Heidegger, it wasn't something that would just happen by itself; he aggressively pursued it like an apostle. When you take something like a cult and try to harness it so that it has political force, this is what you get. Very few people realize that Nazism truly belongs in the category of state churches—or cults, of instances where state and church (religion) were not separate.

"If you want to achieve political goals effectively, you have to simplify things to be clear. You have to have a definable enemy, and simple icons. Cultivating the German cultural spirit is much harder than just getting rid of Jews. Everyone has to have "papers" and papers have to be in order. Racism is the end effect, but not the cause.

"Let me give you an illustration from one of Harlan's state-approved films. Yes, of course, the Jewish character is ruining the social situation and maybe the economy for Germans. But GOLDEN CITY is saying something just as important to note: that the country dweller, the farmer family is pure, while those who are in the city are scandalous. This is just as much part of the view as the anti-semitism, but when is the last time you heard that Nazis were organic farmers who romanticized the life of small towns? Freiberg, where Heidegger taught, was considered the 'goat hills' of Germany, but preferred exactly for that reason.

"So I also want you to see one other thing: that Heidegger is true about his movement. In a sense, 'technology' (systematization) did ruin it—if 'ruin' means to make it obnoxious and dangerous to others by imposing it. They (Heidegger and others who never rejected Nazism) seemed to have copied Christianity in this by more recently turning to *persuasion*. It manifests as environmentalism and liberalism. So their favorite enemy to target is conservatives, which includes presenting Nazism as conservative, to cover up any connection, when in fact the connection is vast. Today's existentialism presents itself as likeable, as devoted to nature, and tolerant. And usually you'd never know from it that Heidegger had a history.

"But today's academia and media are imposition disguised *as* persuasion. So much of the West hinges on

91

Heidegger's axiom that 'intelligibility is suicide for philosophy.' Repeat that 1000 times, and you will have imposed Heidegger's cover-up. His equation is true of Nazi philosophy, which he never left. That's why he wants no one to backtrack him to his days of 'young Germany.' But when you make it intelligible you realize what can happen to the West, if persuasion by reasoning disappears, by this thing or something else like Islam."

Karin interrupted: "Did you hear, then, about the FBI poster, the changed wording about the 'honor killing' suspect—"

"Oh, yes. That would make it intelligible, you see. Islam is another force which must impose or die. No one is supposed to know this about Islam."

"Well, why is that?"

"It discredits or undercuts the two most powerful tenets of Christianity, which have kept the West alive. My interest is purely practical; I'm not here to preach. But, relative to 'intelligibility,' Nazism and Islam are equally opposed. A geometry student might say 'equidistantly' since they are not identical."

"Wow. I need air."

"Right. Let's go for a walk, and get you to your place. Enough on this for now! I can make it back in time for the boys' return. I wonder what *they* were taught today?"

The conflict with CVC did come to a head. Gorden didn't have to do anything beyond that initial meeting. The RCMP and the telecommunications commission held a press conference together. The commission explained the fines and disciplinary actions against the station, and explained that spokespersons would be available to other networks for interviews on the issue.

Karin picked up a copy of the PORT for that day as the story was carried on the front page. "Congratulations, boss!" she announced as she held the newspaper out for Gorden at the café.

But Gorden was not as excited as expected.

"Well, come on, Gorden, their *putsch* was unsuccessful, thanks to you!" She was referring to an incident in Munich in 1933 in which the early Nazi leaders 'got away' with an election irregularity that was small in itself, but just enough to help them emerge.

"Or maybe not 'thanks to me.' I was half-hoping for the chance to make a statement about the station. CVC is an investment of the same Austrian financial management which set up the high-quality production corporation in Germany for the Reich."

Karin gasped and collapsed into her chair. "I can't believe... How did you ever find that out?"

"The small world of the vast internet. I don't see where the connection was made to participating in violent nature, because 'the meltdown' I keep mentioning would happen. So yes, they were caught on this one, but so much more could have been exploited about it with these facts."

"How about holding your own press conference?"

"I was thinking about it, but people really need the one-two punch, and the 'two' would be the extended booklist. It's just not ready. I'll have to find something to feature when it is ready. We'll see."

Karin stored that thought away. She began to think about how Hallon's intervention could be brought up all over again at his own press conference and connected to the booklist with a concise statement about anti-Christian nature movements and their effect on society.

"Guess who I saw near my place this morning?" Gorden asked.

Nothing came to mind.

Gorden got up from the café table and looked up and down the street. "Just as I thought."

"What?" asked Karin. "What's just as you thought?"

"The mandolin player."

"I didn't notice him today."

"That's because he was near my place this morning."

When Gorden returned home, three people came at him from their car before he could get to the front door. A camera was rolling.

"Dr. Hallon, where is your Ph.D. from?"

"CVC?" Gorden countered.

"So what?" fired back a defensive voice.

"Come to the next monthly workshop on the extended booklist."

Silent media hounds are really amusing. Much more than silent hounds.

Sonia opened the front door. "Charles called me from school, and said there was something kicking him in the gut."

Gorden spun around in surprise. Cameras flashed at Sonia behind Gorden.

"Are you part of the household? How many women are there here? Are there any underage girls?"

Sonia was shocked. "What is going on?"

Gorden tried to calm her. "Thank you so much for taking care of Charles. Uhhh, why don't you wait inside while I--, I mean 'til these people are gone?" Turning to the three from CVC he dismissed them, "Well, as you can see I have a sick child, and need to go. Yes, one of you is welcome to attend the next

94

workshop because we appreciate how your coming knocks off all the rust from how we put things we're trying to express."

"So is she the boy's mother? Or is his mother the one you meet over at the Café Montage?"

"Workshop!" fired back Gorden. "Admit one." He took out his card for them. Send an email and I'll get you the time and place."

It was all over the CVC evening edition, which meant it would be in the paper the next morning. And so it was:

CRACK ANTI-ENVIRONMENTALIST
AND HOLOCAUST-DENIER
IN AFFAIRS WITH A NEST OF WOMEN

"Well," laughed Gorden, "you know what that means?"

Karin countered. "Yeah, it means they don't have anything."

"What else?"

"Where did they come up with the 'holocaust-denier' bit?"

"I know. You change any little piece of the established phraseology and they go beserk. You know what we could do is counter that they are the holocaust-deniers—remember, about the 'offering'? That would really hit the fan! What else?"

Karin stared at the paper. "Uhhh…they've become a tabloid."

"Right. Just what we wanted! Annoying, but they're done for."

"Think they'll come?"

"To the workshop? Nah. They're in a different gear; they want something sexy or 'religulous', and they'll never get it. I'll send them a copy of the booklist, though... Strange how they bombard you with sexual questions, when they show whole programs championing anything but committed marital heterosexuality, and think they are mighty explorers for that."

"Well, I can see where that bombardment is maybe decoy number two, if decoy number one is all their notices against racism."

"That's perceptive, Karin. Maybe that's why the Washington State legislature said it was 'historic' to approve same-sex marriage. *Historic?* When things are historic, we know what transpired. We have no idea what this will do. Wreckless maybe, but a-historic in the history department. It's a sort of national debt time-bomb all over again. Not that they know what that amounts to."

Jordan found that construction permission was being slowed until the mind was numb, and there was no money coming in. He was about to risk it all. He had worked his way up in the ranks of the Oregon Builders Association, and had decided it was time they propose a counter-moratorium on moratoriums— because almost no one could get any building done, unless you were a huge firm. Most large business was liberal in thinking. What an odd combination, he thought, this gigantic, 'natural' building scenario. This prompted the state department of inspections to require him to attend a meeting.

What was surprising at the meeting was not the muscle they brought to enforce all this; it was a poet-builder character whose whole approach was a mystical-practical spiel about the need to connect to the One in our construction, to stop doing everything "by thought" that was out of connection to the One.

They insisted that those who see the piles of regulations as dictatorial have simply not attained.

It was coming fast and thick now, and Jordan backed up a step or two. "Attained…what?"

"It has no name. A name would ruin it, as our way of building now does already, for the most part. As a popular poet from the last century said,

'We are always looking at nature / but not from it.'

As though we were separate!"

As he looked around the room, Jordan realized that they had all "attained." This was why none of them questioned the artist-builder.

"OK," he sighed. "Let me ask you a couple questions." He started with the administrator on his right. "How many hours are you at the office with Mr. Zoes, as opposed to in the field?"

"*In* the field? We're not in the field, at all. The 'field' to us is the cases that *come* in for inspection review."

"Allright, and when you're spending all that time in the office, how much time with Mr. Zoes?"

"Well, of course, the whole reason we're with him is that further analysis would miss the connection."

"The *connection*?"

"We're not there to move a building project along…"

"Yes, I kind of knew that!"

"We're there to wait and transform. He has shown us time and again that we can't keep moving things forward in a production line, that we have to look for the connection to the One. That is not ordinary thinking."

97

"How does this happen? I mean is there a book, or what? And what about the customer?"

"There are hours when we don't do anything. It is a matter of inspiration, and no one has it like he has."

"Hours!!! And what does he do? This sounds like what John Denver said about Eckhardt and EST. I mean for crying out loud, does he have a set of blueprints in front of him or a desk or what?"

"I'm not sure there's a word for it, I mean for the vacant spells, but the inspiration, wow!, there's nothing like it!"

"*Vacant spells*! What are you talking about? And this is a publically-funded position, and you all are sitting in a room watching this guy and his vacant spells and then you jump when he's inspired! Well, I'm setting up a press conference, that's what I'm doing. This, this is just 'fundamental transformation of America'! Do you know--you know what capitalism is? Capitalism is what happens when you leave people alone and let them do a transaction."

Zoes was quiet.

"So you're not going to say anything! Who do you think we are?"

Zoes nodded back to the administrator on Jordan's right.

That administrator tried to answer. "Jordan, look, I'm going to make it clear that we're not religious, allright? We're... we believe all reality is one; it's nature. There are no souls. Saying that should make it clear that we're not—that this is not some sort of New Age spirit clique."

"Why are you saying this?"

"Well, we believe that our movement never reached its true potential, because...of mechanization, because of technology."

"Your movement? Oh, I get it. Zoes is the One!"

Zoes was suddenly animated and spoke again which created a buzz among all the administrators because without them--and Jordan--realizing it, he had gone vacant right there in front of Jordan. "But there is no point in naming the movement. Nothing works. It just perpetuates the problem we're in."

"And the public might damn well disagree! But wait a second—'the problem we're in'—what are you talking about?"

"Well, you're a little late, son, if you don't realize the extent of the damage, at this point."

"Damage...to the earth? You know, if you could just stop speaking in riddles, I might be able to work with you. You think you see all kinds of damage, but did you know that by smartthinking about the use of resources, with or without this— this *One*—"and he glared at Zoes "we can now build a house using 5% of the dimensional lumber it took 20 years ago? 5%! Meanwhile, in Germany they have been working on green energy for 25 years and still produce less than half a percent of what's needed!"

"But like I said" answered Zoes with surprising quickness "if you try to name it, you lose it. It's suicide."

And with that Jordan had had enough. His psychic muscles were screaming in pain, if that's what it was that had been working so hard. He could not imagine being in the room a minute longer, and besides there was an assistant manager at a bank he was supposed to have called by now.

"Just so we understand each other, Mr. Zoes," Jordan stood to shake hands and leave, "The moratorium appeal is on."

Zoes had one of those public smiles ready, and when Jordan was out of view, his face grew vacant, the kind of vacancy his staff was all too familiar with.

99

"You'll have to tell all this to Gorden. He's been working on an issue that's a bit heavier, but all the same…"

Jordan, Karin and Gorden were then altogether at the very same table where Karin and Gorden first met months ago.

Karin held Jordan's hand. Gorden noticed and smiled and anticipated.

"We haven't set the date yet!"

"I wish you much happiness. Karin is a great student and made quite a contribution to how the extended booklist works. Now, tell me about the friction with the department of construction, was it?…"

Jordan brought them up to date. "I don't think this Zoes guy realizes where this can go, and is awfully naïve. When I hiked a lot, I knew people who would go to dangerous areas and had this maddening love for nature's capricious ways. If the place was marked as 'subject to extreme weather' they'd charge into it and just laugh defiantly about it, as though we accept everything nature sends and don't take precautions for ourselves or our friends."

"As though nature were a completely innocent thing now, no matter what" added Karin.

"Yeah, so why does Zoes quote that poetry as though all nature ever did was nice or as though we accept everything it does as divinely-ordained? He thinks he's talking about nature, but with all the labyrinth of permits and inspections he's actually talking about human organization and design!"

"Yes, it gets really murky. Irrational. Contradicted," declared Gorden.

"It gets unpredictably *expensive*, which means to me that they are 'handling' nature—this Natural Mandate stuff—to shut down the economy. Meanwhile--have you seen it?—they are funding things like the posters on the bio-diesel buses:

100

CELEBRATE EARTH DAY ALL YEAR
THE EVOLUTION OF GOING GREEN

In which evolution equals practical, calculated economic decisions, which it has never, *ever* meant before. Let's all have fun with evolution and Heckel."

Karin corrected: "*Haeckl.*"

"Right" Jordan acknowledged.

"Well, otherwise people will think you're talking about a character in a gothic novel or something…'

"Oh, right," Jordan agreed.

"Well, about the artist-supervisor," Gorden progressed, "here's a little thing to compare from Heidegger. He had a meeting planned of several professors, brought them all to Freiburg. I'm sure they were all planning on a lecture or presentation in a fine room on campus. Instead, he had them all dropped off in the city so they would *walk* to his simple, peasanty home outside Freiburg for the seminar on Germanness in education. Not even transport them there and back. They were all to wear the uniform of the student association. So he really meant for them to be *Landers*—intimately in contact with the soil--and really meant for it to be formal—in uniform! I have as much problem grasping that as you have your Zen-supervisor, except that I know the 'center' is missing."

"Exactly," replied Jordan.

"So Jordan," Karin added, to get to some practicalities, "I will be finishing the thesis, and then applying around the area for part-time positions introducing all this. We have such an educational curve to surmount. But Gorden's bibliography will go a long ways on that."

"The *area*? You mean to stay here?" He was still flustered by what he'd realized about the mandate and talked himself into some doubts.

"No, no." Karin pulled his hand close to her. "You're really missing me. Home. Portland. There's got to be something. And it's part-time because I have no illusions about what I can do. I'm not going to just show up at home after work, arriving at the same time you do each day, mirroring you as you come home to your haven. I'm going to make it a living home, radiant as an fireplace, fragrant with real, hand-made food, always there for our children. This is how I've resolved it. This is what I can do. Some hours at a college, yes, but they'll never be in the way, do you see?"

"She's done very well regarding all this, Jordan. You've done very well, letting her find her niche in this. The smartest thing you could have done, I think. And she's helped accumulate the material that will be needed to establish—or retrieve—the core beliefs needed at this time in our culture. I appreciate very much your part in the sacrifice for it."

5: JUST PERFECT
FOR WRITING PHILOSOPHY

The kind of silence with which Karin was welcomed in to Dr. Pritchett's office was saying more than she wanted. This was her second try in the Portland area where she had at least some promising initial response. It didn't help that another administrator was waiting there seated, and Karin was unaware there was to be anyone else.

"Now, let's begin by saying that the work you've done is impressive. We cannot deny this. But the committee has decided against the course. I've asked a colleague and advisor to the committee to summarize the reasons."

The woman introduced herself as Dr. Lissy Patella. "There are two reasons, and I'll be brief. First, that we could find no interest in the subject in any of the usual areas where we look. You'd have done yourself a favor with a class on denial of the Holocaust, or the rise of Neo-Nazism in America, and you have the background for that. Second, we find that such an emphasis as you did take would be more than controversial. By that, we mean, that you would not have something that was part of the necessary general debate that needs to take place in this country for it to thrive intellectually. Instead you have something that can only go one place, and we therefore cannot see it fostering a climate of discovery, challenge, and genuine inquiry."

Karin was jarred, and this silence was worse than the previous. "Tell me something then. Where do you think a course like this belongs?"

Dr. Pritchett answered. "What we really think is that you need to find something that conforms to the 'natural mandate.' What you have here would erase 100 years of progress and concensus-building."

Karin objected, "But doesn't that just have to do with construction? My husband's a builder and always running into it, almost to the point where he has no work."

"It's about all of life."

"All of life? Really? Can I just say, that I won't be offended at all if you want to criticize my research for being Christian, even though I say that perfunctorily, meaning, I'm not preaching Christianity from the inside, but I'm describing its contributions as a social observer—or show what happens when it's fundamentally opposed? But you see, that's not even what this is about, and I've caught you off-guard. I have broken through clichés and images, and have stated clearly that when you have all these anti-Christian elements inter-breed, you get what happened there in 'young Germany.'

"You know, it's not that hard to compare Islam's monotheism with West Coast Buddhism as systems of thought and realize that they are irreconcilable. So in this course, you have all these elements, you can see they are anti-Christian, and

104

you can also see that they are the *modus operandi* culturally today—they are the 'nature mandate'—and even the denial of this is getting to be silly. What you've encountered is not someone here to preach Christianity, but to demonstrate anti-Christianity, except that the person speaking loves goodness, and instead of seeing an awful situation like Yeats in 'The Second Coming,' you've just written it off! Like—what did you say—it 'wouldn't foster inquiry, challenge, discovery'? What in the world?

"I know you don't want to discuss religion any further than you can help it, but in this case, you'd just be saying these people woke up one morning and decided Jews were the problem and organized to liquidate them. If you do that, you'll be *crushing* 'inquiry, challenge, discovery'! Just go flip through the booklist. And that's where Heidegger wanted it—unintelligible! And I think I know *why*."

The very rattled representatives of the college then complimented Karin on her passion, but subjected her to a polite, verbal treatment that she didn't have a handle for. It was the enormous pile of guilt—for not concensus-building. After a while Karin didn't hear them, but she did return to what the woman had said about the matter of 'only going one place.' '*So they know!*' Karin thought to herself, 'or it's just so omnipresent that they don't know they are *in* it.'

"Well, I accept your decision, but let me tell you something that would happen if I held this course, because it has to do with your belief that groups should not be offended."

"And what is that?" asked Patella, trying to sound bored.

"People would gather around and ask for it to be stopped because it is offending the *subject* of the course. And guess who that is?" She picked up her rejection letter and her leather case and moved to the door. "A good day to you both," and she left.

105

Pritchett and Patella absorbed what they had just heard, not meeting eyes, just pondering.

"Well," said Patella finally, "we did everything by the book. There's a lot of wisdom in avoiding structurally-offensive language."

It was now a year since Karin had returned from Vancouver. She had been able to set up one class at Portland State, but was getting the strangest looks from other professors and sometimes from students. There were rumors it would not be repeated. It had been offered on a contingency basis; if approved, it would be an elective for credit for various BA programs. She felt a bit guilty like she was asking them to learn another language, but hadn't told them that.

"That's not far off," Gorden reassured her. "I've been waiting for you to run into this, to feel this. You know, you might be able to save your spot there by describing it that way."

"Do you think so?" Karin felt recharged at the sound of his voice, even by phone.

"Remember when I talked about you being opposed and hounded, and how you needed to know these things for yourself. Well, here we are and this is how you're doing."

"Well, it's not very well."

"I think I can tell you this now, and you will see it. The iconography that has been built up, the simple anti-semitism, the hate by the Nazis—this is all a stronghold of perceptions to make them seem so irrational, so out of nowhere. Anything but the intellectual leaders of their day. I'll bet anything you have people telling you they know what the Nazis were about when they say they were anti-semitic and so forth."

"Only every day. But it's not an answer. It doesn't get inside their heads, it doesn't plumb the depths. Hating is not a reason, it's the *result* of something else. Or things."

"Of what?" Gorden asked her to assess how fluent she was on the topic.

"This is it, Gorden; this is what baffles and intrigues me about this topic—to this day. As a granddaughter as well as a researcher. Why can't people take the next step?"

"Uh-huh. It's the stronghold."

"And what do you mean by that?"

"I don't want to preach and you know I've been reserved about the anti-Christianity which it clearly is. But a stronghold is a mass mental block, and paradigm filter—what can I say? In Christianity, it is an explanation why people don't believe, or don't like goodness. Someone, a media force, etc., has done an awfully good job at making it the 'air' people breathe. They don't know anything else. So I will give you two quick responses to your question. One is the big picture and the other is a small detail."

"The big picture actually comes from a child of that generation, a German Christian, whose Ph.D. dissertation was on Marx. There is a line there about dictatorships that will blow away the fog. Listen:

If you try to enforce a rule through the civil administration, then you find that you are on the way to a tyranny. Today we see a whole list of environmentalists and critics of development on this path... When there is no longer a proper (individual) responsibility, then a country is not able to be ruled except by a dictator.

"That says a lot, coming from someone raised in it!"

"So he knew!" Karin observed.

107

"I don't think he sees an individual dictator out there today, though, that's why he says there's a 'whole list.' The small detail is the moment when Heidegger had all the regional college deans to his place. You may remember the story. He had them arrive in the city and dropped off at an office, but then he made them walk out to the meeting place at his house in the country. Now these are all professionals, and one would be off to Milan the next week and another to New York. But Heidegger had them walk two miles through the fields to his house to actually be in contact with the motherland, the soil. What kind of people make demands like this? Think about it."

"Yeah, I see what you mean. Thanks for taking the time again. The students who don't see it--I can understand. It's my colleagues. It's the 'corporate culture' where there is so much praise for each other, but are they really capable of taking on a tough question?"

"Well, they're not," answered Gorden quicker than Karin expected. "Let me read you something about peers taking a tough question. It's something Gasman said about Haeckel:

In West Germany a major conference on Haeckel, organized in 1978 by the Association of German Societies for the History of Medicine, gave expression to a widely held opinion in that country, when it set out to run determined interference against the idea that Haeckel, the enlightened, progressive, secular, and above all materialist thinker could be associated with mysticism and the genesis of National Socialism.

"Yeah, there's interference alright."

"Karin, I treat you as my disciple, and I think you understand that. So let me tell you my two conclusions about all this, and my fear for the West, because I just saw it on a bumper sticker."

"Wait a second." Karin knew it was going to be forcefully put. "I want notes...OK, ready."

"The whole movement really is the logical and practical result of anti-Christianity. I've summarized that. But to see that, you have to agree to accept the truth of what you've observed. So here is the problem. I went for a walk this week, and came along a car with a bumper sticker that I'm afraid states the mentality of the West more than I would ever have liked. Just two words:

DENY EVERYTHING

"If we do that, if we go that direction, I can't imagine what will happen. You'd go against objective information, and again, not to preach, but I've listened to the better Christian thinkers, and they all say something like 'all truth is God's truth' or 'God communicates a unified message both inside and outside the revealed Scripture' or something like that. In other words, they don't 'deny everything.'

"I've been trying to imagine. I think what it sets up is a world of affirmers of objective truth versus those who deny it. There's something powerful about denial; you get that feeling of *control*, like you can get back or gain back something major that was lost, that you are angry about. I think about Speer saying 'Hitler had the uncanny ability to get us to feel so sorry for all the unfair things that had happened to him'.

"But about this—do you see it? A culture opposed to objective information? Opposed to intelligibility? In the detail of what you've studied here: do you see a culture developing that is opposed to realizing that a people can think of themselves so essentially a part of nature that they dictate it on to the rest— because of another denial, that is, that nature can be harsh, unfair, destructive? And they can demean or dismiss or disenfranchise those they have determined are not worth being alive?"

Karin shuddered. "I'm afraid you're right. I can't take any more right now, OK? And I pray like everything that you're wrong."

"Well, there is something else, and it won't be heavy; in fact, it will be fascinating; it will bring some closure, which will be very settling for you."

"Yeah? What's that?"

"I'm sure you know who Rachel Carlson is."

"SILENT SPRING, etc."

"Correct. Well, her campaign against DDT was signed into law by President Nixon, but her goal was a global ban, you know."

"Gorden, you said this was upbeat..."

"Well, we're pretty sure that the number of deaths in Africa due to malaria, due to the ban on DDT there, is 100 million. With an M."

Karin gasped. "Uhh, you *did* say this was upbeat."

"Right. Well, the first day you saw me was in Portland at that hotel. After the workshop, I wanted to speak with that 'distant cousin' of yours. He'd said something very glossy about all these environmental plans as though they always work out just as dreamt. That man with the German accent who drinks Beck's and who had the friend with him. Not that I know that for sure he was your cousin, but it turns out you have the same name. Yeah, that was me. I just explained to him how some of these environmental side-effects work, and about Rachel Carlson."

"That's right! So *that's* what that was about, that heated exchange. Oh, I'll have to try to look him up and see where he's

110

at now. I can tell this work and this topic has overloaded me; I never even asked you about being there this whole time. Wow, so that is what happened?"

"Heated? Oh, yes, yes. On *their* side. Global warming, you know!"

Karin laughed. "Got to keep your sense of humor!"

"Yeah, his world fell apart. And I didn't even get to tell him about the EPA's tests on people with toxic fumes, which is a legal action now."

The phone rang while Karin was housecleaning with a vengeance. She could only tell from her screen that it was a local Portland number.

"Yes, Karin, we noticed on your resume that you were related to Heidegger's assistant, and are quite impressed with the work you've done. We'd like to offer you a part-time position with an option for Ph.D. studies in exchange."

Karin gasped. "I don't know what to say! Amazing! What would you like me to do next?..."

When she had taken down notes and hung up, she flopped on her bed, but in fact felt like she was floating, in a balloon over waves of grass, bowing in the wind. "Oh, my goodness, oh, my..."

She dialed Jordan and then she was going to call Gorden. "Honey, can you stop for a minute and listen? A college has called, and they've offered me something higher than I expected..."

"You mean you're high-ered? You know? Get it?"

* * *

111

Heidegger was comfortably relaxing at his foothill lodge in the Black Forest. Death Mountain, as a name for the place, took some getting used to, but you just had to think in terms of what he was trying to end, or put to death. He was now professor emeritus of philosophy.

His wife asked, "Dear, are you still thinking about how the Allied administration thinks of you as 'running along with the herd' — a *Mitlaufer*?"

"No, no. I've got used to that." He looked around the landscape of their neighborhood and the perfectly-kept Black Forest that defined some of their horizon, actual and spiritual. "I think this is just the perfect *raum* in which to write philosophy. And anyway I did help those Jewish girls escape."

His wife tensed. "We said we weren't going to talk about them anymore."

German glossary

Aryosophy: Aryan theosophy; a popular new biological and organically-German view of the world. Its esoteric spirituality was peripheral and perhaps annoying to some Germans; at its core, it was the same doctrines as the main thinkers held in their effort to supply a uniquely German cosmology and nature-religion

Aufklarung: a mental breakthrough, an illumination

Existentialismus: Existentialism. To quote Dr. Schaeffer in THE GOD WHO IS THERE: "A modern theory of man that holds that human experience is not describable in scientific or rational terms. Existentialism stresses the need to make vital choices by using man's freedom in a contingent and apparently purposeless world." Schaeffer spoke at the University of Freiburg in 1967 on "faith vs. 'faith'" (Christian vs. existentialist), Heidegger's main subject there in previous decades.

Kampf: the struggle to dominate; for Germans, the struggle to dominate the planet as the one truly natural species.

Machtenshaft: to mechanize things that are otherwise spontaneous or fluid.   Heidegger wished that the monistic movement of 'young Germany' had not mechanized. The Reich's swastika itself appears to be a symbol that was mechanized—it appears to be rigid and ominous, yet includes the creative force of the Hindu symbol. This is intended to convey that destruction is creation.

Materialism (philosophic): the view that there is no divine action or interaction in the universe, nor has been in the past, nor in the future.

Mitlaufer: literally 'those who run with the wagon' which is bringing in the harvest or the meat from the annual hunt. It was a status applied to certain Germans after the war who did not appear to have full membership in the Nazi party.

Monismus: Monism. The biologically-based belief that there was only one reality, nature, and Germans were part of that.

Lebensraum: "Living space." The name for geographic areas Nazi Germany believed to be theirs for the expansion of the one people who were one piece with nature.

Putsch: an attempt to seize power or leverage out of a situation beyond what a group or party would normally have

Volk, -isch: The people mentioned above.

Wandervogel: The wandering birds, a 'mascot' name for the German youth generation who were adrift between World Wars and disenchanted with much of modern society.

Wehrmacht: Military

Weltanschauung: A view of the world; a philosophy.

29772037R10067

Made in the USA
Charleston, SC
24 May 2014